LAST PERFORMANCE AT THE ODEON

LAST PERFORMANCE AT THE ODEON

Being the memoirs of a Jewish woman growing up in Britain – Kibbutz, Love, Death and the search for her Romanian roots

CAROL SUSAN NATHANSON

MAIDA VALE PUBLISHING

First published in 2018
by Maida Vale Publishing Ltd
Suite 333, 19-21 Crawford Street
Marylebone, London W1H 1PJ
United Kingdom

Cover design and typeset by Edwin Smet
Printed in England by TJ International Ltd, Padstow, Cornwall

ISBN 978-1-912477-61-6

MIX
Paper from
responsible sources
FSC® C013056
FSC
www.fsc.org

WWW.EYEWEARPUBLISHING.COM

To my mother,
to my children

Carol Susan Nathanson
has completed the Graduate Diploma in Writing with Commendation at The National Academy of Writing, and an Honours Degree in Performance Arts. Her prose poetry has been published in anthologies and performed at Foyles in London and Birmingham City University. Carol has lived on kibbutz, raised a family and worked in the theatre. More recently, she worked as a Consultant Adult Psychotherapist for the NHS.

The title of the story refers to the last performance of prayers at the Odeon, Temple Fortune. It was used as a synagogue overflow every year for the Day of Atonement Services. It was my cinema.

For the protection of privacy, certain individuals' names have been changed.

TABLE OF CONTENTS

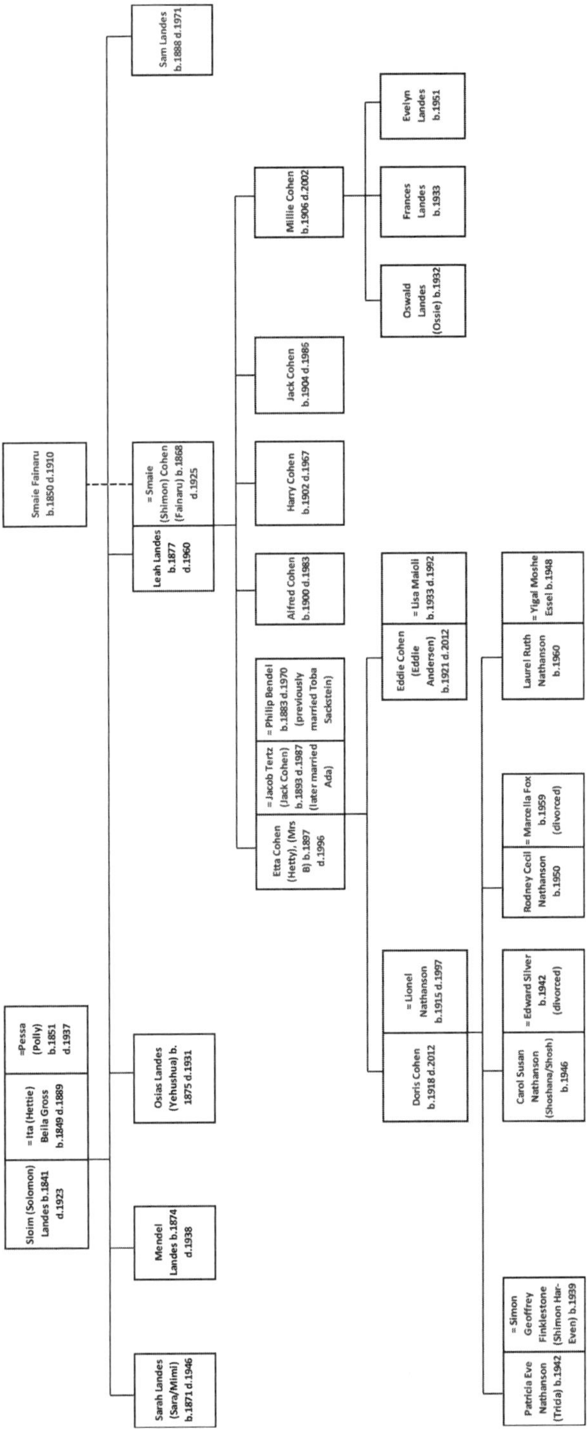
Smaie Fainaru b.1850 d.1910
Sloim (Solomon) Landes b.1841 d.1923
= Ita (Hettie) Beila Gross b.1849 d.1889
=Pessa (Polly) b.1851 d.1937
Sarah Landes (Sara/Mimi) b.1871 d.1946
Mendel Landes b.1874 d.1938
Osias Landes (Yehushua) b. 1875 d.1931
Leah Landes b.1877 d.1960
= Smaie (Shimon) Cohen (Fainaru) b.1868 d.1925
Sam Landes b.1888 d.1971
Etta Cohen (Hetty), (Mrs B) b.1897 d.1996
= Jacob Tertz (Jack Cohen) b.1893 d.1987 (later married Ada)
= Philip Bendel b.1883 d.1970 (previously married Toba Sackstein)
Alfred Cohen b.1900 d.1983
Harry Cohen b.1902 d.1967
Jack Cohen b.1904 d.1986
Millie Cohen b.1906 d.2002
Oswald Landes (Ossie) b.1932
Frances Landes b.1933
Evelyn Landes b.1951
Doris Cohen b.1918 d.2012
= Lionel Nathanson b.1915 d.1997
Eddie Cohen (Eddie Andersen) b.1921 d.2012
= Lisa Maloli b.1933 d.1992
Patricia Eve Nathanson (Tricia) b.1942
= Simon Geoffrey Finklestone (Shimon Har-Even) b.1939
Carol Susan Nathanson (Shoshana/Shosh) b.1946
= Edward Silver b.1942 (divorced)
Rodney Cecil Nathanson b.1950
= Marcella Fox b.1959 (divorced)
Laurel Ruth Nathanson b.1960
= Yigal Moshe Essel b.1948

SAGA ROSE

Saga Rose
slides through the water like a bird
fallen.

I want to be alone, not moving, to stand under the hull
of the ship and feel her
grandeur; to know that she is bigger than me.
She docks at the foot of a steep black mountain.
Water laps onto slabs of rock and
there is a quiet, only broken by gentle gusts of breeze
and strong waves folding
themselves over and over again onto grit and stone,
pebble and leaf. Across the
water, not the impending black shadows of stone and crag,
owned for centuries by the glaciers of
Norway, but instead, silver grey boulders coated with
heather and moss,
reaching out to blue grey sky with tufts of cloud.
Perfect stillness, quietness; a place where fragments of my past
can be pulled together.

I like space around me – long views, mountains,
hills and moors.
In the woods I look for the spaces in between,
the clearings that the trees conceal.
I like separateness rather than the herd.[1]

★

I grew up in between.
We were four:
Patricia, Carol, Rodney
and Laurel.

Patricia, Rodney and Carol as children

In the background stood a family of merchants, beginning with the master baker, Mr Smaie Fainaru, living in Romania at the end of the nineteenth century, his hardworking son Shimon and his obedient wife, Leah, and two of their children, Hetty and Alf – one born beneath the rafters of a flour mill at the top of a hill in Dorohoi, and the other at the bottom of the stairs, just under the banisters of a haberdashery shop in Islington, overrun with rats and the smell of pickled herrings.

Migrating Jews had been clambering onto the decks of steamers since the early nineteenth century; their diaspora was clogged up with poverty, disease and persecution.

They needed to find a home
as I did.

Carol in the mountains

IN BETWEEN

The pavements overflowed with Jews dressed in smart, fashionable clothes bought specially for the occasion. There is almost no traffic on the roads. It is strange. The women are stepping out in time with their husbands; no handbags to clutch, no coins to be counted, no more carp or herring to be chopped, no kreplach *to be stuffed, no more bread to be sliced, no potato* kugel *to be baked, no rice to be rinsed. In every home, the table is laid. The cloth is clean. The candlesticks polished. The evening meal, prepared for after sunset. Today is* Yom Kippur.

Mrs Polonsky waves to my father. He has a soft spot for her. He walks over to her, fingering his moustache and stroking his hair. He smiles, even touches her arm. My father is handsome. He likes to flirt with the ladies. For after all, she is still in her prime. I remember her loud voice. She used to shriek. My mother stands alone and says nothing. The crowd gathers together, pushing and shoving their way into the cinema, squeezing their bodies onto narrow seats, the men unfolding their prayer shawls, opening the machzor*: will they be granted another year of life? Will I?*

They turn their heads to peer at the women, savouring this moment before the curtains go up; before the lights go down. The haunting melody of Kol Nidrei *echoes in my memory. It is atonement.*

Will you love, honour, comfort and cherish her
from this day forward
forsaking all others?

When I read these words, I think about my mother. I imagine she hoped they would be true. I know when it was my turn, I thought the promise would last forever, like a foreign kingdom bequeathed to a princess. But the story didn't quite work out like that. Everything changes.

Doris and Lionel, 3rd November 1940

AS IT DID WITH JACK
Born in Poland of a different name –
Jacob Terz
fled from Hetty in Chapel Street and married Ada
who would have believed it –
the shop girl from America.

Jack Cohen born Jacob Terz, makes a new life in America after abandoning his family in England.

High up on the hills of Safed, in the half-light of a biblical dawn, my sister Patricia opens the door of her cellar, stands on her tiptoes and pulls down from a

dusty shelf a rusty old metal box. She yanks it open; extracts a brown envelope, torn in three corners. She swallows hard, mumbles under her breath.
Found them.

November 1940
Jack Cohen writes to Lionel:

Hello Nathanson,

I hope you are in the very best of health. Many thanks for your letter, and may I stress the point, here and now, how pleased I am that you were introduced to me. According to the photographic appearance, I take you to be worthy of my daughter, Doris, in marriage. As a father, I hope that you will always be very happy together, and always stick together: the main thing in marriage is to be united in love or business, barriers or journeys should not matter; try, and you must, not to be out of each other's sight. I am then confident that all will be well. May God guide you both and as you know there is God in each one of us, so cheer up and have the optimistic view of life and be happy.

My position I had already explained to my Doris, but I will do all I can for both of you in the near future, as they say better late than never –

Now, my dear Nathanson, the way you plead in your letter about Eddie certainly adds salt to my wounds, but I am an old timer and guess I can take it. One more tragedy in my lifetime does hurt but I can get over it. You see, my boy Eddie might be bad in everyone's eyes, but to me he is my son. God has no temper upon all his children in this world, and neither have I against my only son, I love him, but cannot get near him. Nevertheless I know he needs kindness, sympathy, someone to understand him and heal his wounds. He may be undesirable to all-comers, but to me he is my loving child, unfortunate for him that he did not have the guidance of a loving father, so you see Nathanson, if you want to do me a kindness, I mean when you can (I know you are in the army), talk to him in a kindly manner, show no temper, find out what his real weaknesses are, and in that channel-line, you will find out actually what is in his mind, surely there must be a way to understand him. As you know, there is so much good in the worst of us. Please do not allow anyone to slander his name, do not allow anyone to call him bad bad bad, until you have convinced yourself that your trying efforts have failed –

It is very tragic, but a way must be found, and please give him every opportunity. I am confident he will come through. Punishment of severity is no earthly use if by common logic the objective fails, so bear with me and treat him mildly but firmly. He might realise his error. Tell me in your next letter how far progress had been made if you please.

I had one letter from him about two months ago and gave him my prompt reply, but of course I am still waiting to hear from him. I can assure you he had every consideration and explanation. He also informed me that he is working at a firm called Richards. Well that is good, though a trade in hand is even better than a businessman in his capacity. You see, when a person has a trade in hand, he has a better opportunity in the world, whereas a businessman cannot last unless he has capital. That of course is a matter of opinion. To get back to where we left off, I think that you better tell him that maturity is just round the corner and that parents are only entitled to be his guardian to the age of twenty-one. So he better pull up and be good from now or else.

I know the war is depressing inside or outside it. Anyone that loves England the way I do feels the great sorrow surrounding it, but England has always come through and will with 'god's' help come through again. There will always be an England. May the almighty God bless the dearest people, the King and the beloved Queen and all the royal family.

Well, I close with these words, that God will and shall guide you, and accept my dearest love to you Nathanson and your wife Doris.

Bless you both,
Your father, Jack

1932
Doris, fourteen years old, pulling her bolero tight across her bosom, clutching hold of the lamp post with a tight fist, peers at him, not knowing him, blinking the tears back, having to say goodbye –
Why is he running off to America?
She never sees her father again.

July 28th 1947
Doris receives a letter from her father.

I clearly appreciate receiving the snaps of your daughter Patricia. She looks more or less like you did, except for her blue eyes. Without flattery, she looks wonderful. As for her younger sister, Susan[2]*, I have yet to see what she looks like –*

You know, and this comes from the heart, that I wish you all well and the greatest of happiness.

A father, however brutal he may be, uppermost in his mind are his children and believe me when I say that I had sleepless nights and shed many tears thinking of you and Eddie boy, but if only I could do something, then I would perhaps be in a position to heal my children's wounds.

I am a condemned man. I am in no position to do anything and I dare not go beyond the privileges which are granted to me, for if I overstep or make a blunder now, well I might even become a beggar, particularly if I should cause friction between ourselves here. I wanted to go abroad and start again in business, but the British Consulate did not allow me to obtain a visa, reasons were given that the food and housing problem is at a critical stage. They cannot support their own people, let alone foreigners, so it means that I am stuck for now at least.

I had obtained the American passport for travel and sold everything in the hope of being allowed a visa but it has definitely been blocked and there remains little that I can do. The only people allowed to go to Britain are holidaymakers and they have to be back within three months. So you see I have to settle down all over again and start life anew. My ambitious motives did not prevail. Then you say I look as handsome as ever. I might add that you would be terribly disappointed.

I have changed not only in looks but in habit.

Please Doris do not write to me, until I shall be in a position to let you have an address where we can in future write to each other, so kindly hold it over and until then be patient. I must confess that your letter by registered post had come to my door at the time when I was on my own, and oh boy was I lucky, though I must say your letter did not indicate anything of value if it would have been received by anyone else.

Tell me also how Eddie boy is getting on, is he perhaps engaged to some millionaire's daughter...?

How is your mother? And above all write to me about yourself, your children and your dear husband, Nathanson. Kiss him for me.

I wish you all my very best. I will write as soon as it is permissible. So long Doris dear. All my love.

Yours,
The tyrannical father

August 1947

My dearest daughter Doris,

One day I might send the presents that I owe you all. Then it will be a real surprise. I have not forgotten and I am hoping to fulfil obligations.

Many, many, happy birthdays to baby Susan.

My address now is at 462 Cocran Ave.,
Los Angeles. 36, California.[3]

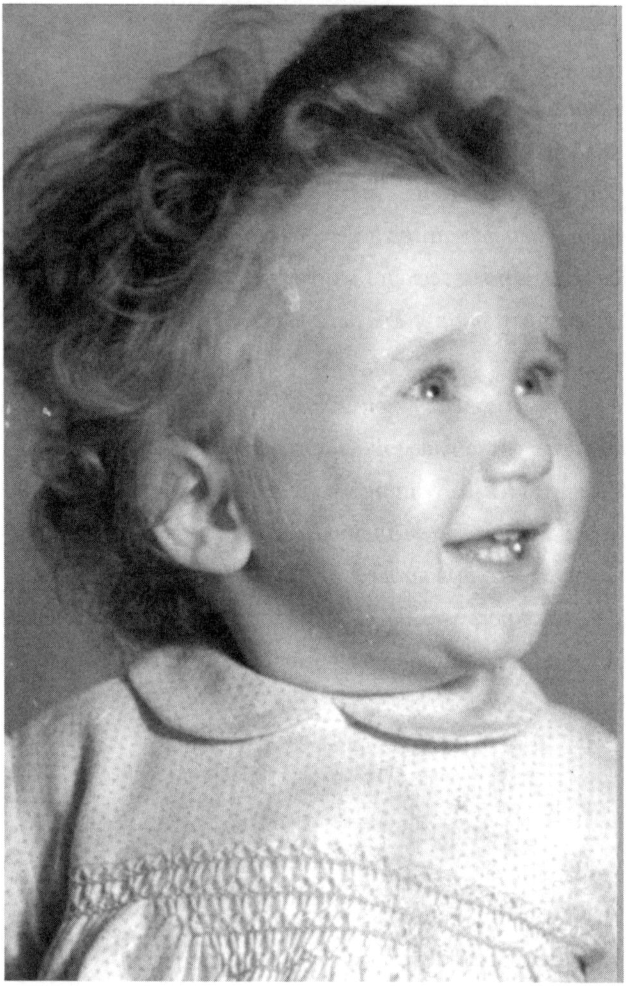

Baby Susan

The fact is our grandfather never set eyes on any of us before you were born, and never enquired after his own great-grandchildren and as to the marriage break-up with Hetty, we never knew any of the details. He ruined Mum's life and Eddie's. So it's hard to feel anything for him.

– *Patricia Har-Even*

*

Poor old Eddie. His father had hammered him, labelling his neglected and abandoned son as 'bad', 'undesirable' and 'tragic', yet all the time referring to the wounds of his children. Perhaps at heart, deep inside, he was a sensitive man. How will any of us know. On the day my parents booked their tickets to Los Angeles, he died. Such is the way of fate –

One story whispered in our ears was that Eddie had been a conscientious objector during the Second World War, infuriating and embittering my father as he tended the broken bodies of British servicemen, or was it merely a case of Eddie failing his call-up papers? Men who wore spectacles could not be trained as soldiers.

And as to academic aspirations, Eddie dropped out. The architectural trainee turned into a draughtsman and on a Saturday morning, at nine a.m. to be precise (ignoring the Sabbath), lifted up his sandwich board and carted around rebellious messages to all and sundry. Chapel Market was invigorated. The tactics of politics could be played out in different ways. He even changed his name in 1944. After all, he didn't want to be identified as a Jew. Hitler might have landed –

EDDIE BOY

Carol places her bottom onto a large squashy sofa in her grandmother's flat, number 49 Cumberland Court. The smell of roast lamb and potatoes drifts in and out of the living room, filled to the brim with mahogany and interwoven with a waft of petrol that filters through an opened sash window – or was it two?

Cars and buses hoot impatiently, the sun goes in and out. Carol doesn't know what to do with herself. She waits with her sister Tricia for lunch.

The key turns in the lock. Uncle Eddie shuffles in. A tall, bespectacled, gentle man – yet odd.

A separate soul.

He begins his story –

Tricia clenches her fist and drums her fingers on the glass coffee table. She needs to go to the toilet but she's scared to interrupt. He speaks of the past. He is softly spoken. Carol sits still, hardly daring to breathe.

'And did you know, I even saw a R101 airship fly over our house in 1930 – crashed in northern France, on its way to India. Remarkable, quite remarkable.'

Carol utters not a word.

Five minutes later Tricia grabs her sister's hand and they follow Eddie to his bedroom, staring avidly at the medley of books and ornaments standing on his mantelpiece. He's been folding paper into exquisite shapes, butterflies, parasols – intricate, delicate.

He is an enigma, Uncle Eddie.

I pick up the bundle of letters that he sent me – one of them folded precisely into a triangle. Eddie stood on the edge of two worlds, like me, between the individual and the collective – abandoned by his father at the age of twelve, he chose to stand apart.

He died 9th July 2012, spectacles propped on his nose.

Mother is glued to a deckchair on the promenade deck of the Saga Rose. It faces south, so at least she'll get some colour on her cheeks. Lately her eyes are failing and she's started to accuse everyone of stealing. But when she was in the bar last night, reminiscing about Dad, I warmed to her.

'You know what Dad was like,' she said, 'always trying to earn a few guineas, dumping hat boxes on the counters, schmoozing all the shopgirls.'

'Yes, I know what he was like.'

With survival dependent upon profiteering from the garment trade, selling long wool coats with fur collars, wedding dresses with huge sleeves for fat *schwartzers*[4] (how I hated the way he described them) and handmade hats and fur muffs for the rich, all hurriedly sewn in the back bedroom of a semi in Tottenham, the moral ethic borne down to me was merely to pick up the pins with an outsize horseshoe magnet and watch Dad flirting with the 'girls' as they covered up the racks of dresses with stained sheets and bid him g'night.

Dad and the girls – The Bargain Shop, 56 Chapel Market, 1950s

I remember their giggles as they took each other's arm and burst out into the smelly dirt of Chapel Market. Stiletto shoes were slung back on, with back straps falling from ankles, angora boleros covering up shoulders. Dad was left behind to stand within the safe confines of a wooden kiosk, writing figures down with a stubby pencil plucked out from behind his ear and trying to work out how much of the day's takings he could safely stuff into a back pocket. And then he'd pick up the long pole, hook it under a ridge and pull the metal shutters down. He was always disappointed – the whole world disappointed him, clasping the Lodge of Joppa notebook close to his chest, one eye on the telephone in case it rang, and one on Mum, checking to see that she wasn't complaining.

Poor old Dad – he'd tried entertaining the

troops in '41, clinging onto the rope for dear life, trying to jump to the other side of the trench, but failing miserably and having to hang there, until some poor sod took pity on him and plonked him back into a mass of nettles on the river bank. No, he wouldn't make the rank of an officer. The name of sergeant would have to suffice, though his stories of running up the mountainside in Monte Cassino handing out plasters and crêpe bandages to the wounded did win the respect of his family.

No, he wouldn't make the rank of an officer. The name of sergeant would have to suffice.

But they got him in the end because the old man was greedy, falling in love with the black market, excited by his entrepreneurship, stuffing notes in his back pocket, throwing them high in the sky into clouds tinged pink by the Jungfrau. He hid it all in Switzerland. Patricia knew about it. I didn't.

★

Mother is losing her memory. Father has died. I remember visiting him in hospital. He was still flirting with the nurses. In the end he sat on a chair beside his bed with catheter inserted, his face in a quiet polite daze, his eyelids closed. He hated it when people kept asking how he was, he wanted to be left alone. But he asked me all right: 'How's the boyfriend?'

He heaves a sigh.

He was still a handsome man. Could have been a film star.

★

My mother is resting in her cabin. Outside, fishing boats are bobbing up and down. I lie back on a sun lounger and squint at the bright sun.

The mountains are majestic, white tips of snow just waiting to be chopped off with a pickaxe. Waterfalls cascade down sheets of sheer black rock. If I'm daring, I could scramble down onto a little pebbly beach enclave, squashed between gushing streams, buttercups and dandelions, pungent, explosive.

But I have to be careful. Ten minutes after brushing breakfast from her lap, Mum plonks herself down in an armchair in front of the dining room, and refuses to move until one of those 'long-haired Norwegian hussies' opens the door. She's lost her aspirin and is being abusive. 'The bitches!' she yells out. I hold my tongue.

It is a very fragile line that exists between hysteria and containment; an abstract thought I know, but one that I understand and know about, because it concerns Mother.

★

I do wish you were here, Laurel. You were always closer to Mum. You knew how to handle her. I rummage in my bag for Laurel's letter. I want to read it again.

When I remember her, we're climbing up a steep hill in the South Downs in Sussex, and chuckling because there at the top of Chanctonbury Hill are three lads starting to pour out tea from a large metal teapot.

'Wow... Perfect, perfect timing,' I shout out and we scramble up, giggling, onto the soft grassy verge alongside some brambles and hawthorn bushes.

'Would you like a cuppa?' one of them says, eying the pretty face and toned body of my younger sister. She has this way of attracting men the moment they catch a first glimpse of her. But she puts on an accent. I grit my teeth.

Yet I loved it when Laurel came to England. She grew up in the suburb, the famous Hampstead Garden Suburb, where ladies of middle-class England found barristers, poets or lawyers to sleep with. Laurel was never short of men. In the end, she too ran away, married and conceived three children in the valley of Jezreel. I shut my eyes. *Feels like yesterday…*

I inhabit two homes, always in between.

★

It is twilight in *Bet Lechem*[5].

The smell of the jasmine is sensual and intoxicating. Laurel grabs hold of her two dogs. We walk together, past elegant Templar houses, built of stone, gardens abundant with anemones and cyclamens. The foliage blends into one dark mass of greenery, stabbing my senses sharply and then drifting away into the distance.

My sister belongs here. I merely dream –

I would need a family to live here; not be on my own. An elderly neighbour stops for a moment to take breath, leaning on her walking stick. Children zoom past on bicycles or scooters. In the morning, when the sun is still down, they clamber noisily onto the school bus. Parents give them yet another kiss and wave goodbye. On Saturdays, those of the faith rush over to the synagogue.

The *moshav* restores a balance inside her,

makes her thankful for what she has. Yet at times she is restless.

I know that feeling. I have battled with it all my life. It is a sense of needing, movement, change. Together, our energy is renewed. We are more hopeful, appreciative. We reminisce. Father is gone, Mother still alive. Dad loved it here, laughing his head off when he'd turn up in surprise, all the way from Chapel Market, ramming on my sisters' door, and thrusting into her arms an enormous pile of kippers and herrings, wrapped up in the *Sunday Times* newspaper.

Chico pulls on the lead. He is a strong animal, suited more to the ice lands than the dried up grasses of Lower Galilee. He discovers a small tortoise behind a bush. He carries it in his mouth, proudly.

We climb to the top of a small enclave and I am twenty years younger, running through a forest of ancient oak trees, summersaulting down a hill and treading carelessly over carpets of buttercups and irises. We shriek in laughter, and clamber over stone and rubble until we reach the Bedouin village of *Ka'abiyya*. The cypress trees and red-roofed houses of *Allone Abba*, a nearby moshav, lie hidden. *Daliat-el Carmel* on the mountains peeps down; *Nazareth* rises up to a blue horizon, its biblical history spread miscellaneously over a hillside that drops into the sea – Laurel, can you really see the sea from there? On a clear day, sis. Ice-blue, shining...

It is pitch black. I venture out with torch in hand. The moon is crescent-shaped, sharp, glistening. I

open the door of my sister's house. A black cat jumps onto the piano. A brown mottled one hides behind a settee. I shoo them away –
I hate cats.
They scare me.
I don't know what they're thinking.
I need to know that.
With everyone.
No more secrets.
Please.

*

I grab the handle of the white transit van, and clamber up, trying not to get my skirt caught around the gear stick. Laurel pushes it upwards aggressively. The sun is already beating down onto my elbow, stuck out through a half-open window. I've smeared suntan cream all over my face and neck, covered my shoulders with an old Arab *kafia* and transferred the clobber of my handbag into a beige string bag, falling apart at the seams.

We build up speed, surging forward on the edge of hairpin bends to a valley, once inhabited by prophets, now desecrated by petrol stations, shopping malls and villages that have neither beginnings or ends.

Laurel walks in front of me. Her legs are strong, shapely and tanned. Blue cotton shorts cover her thighs. She showed them to me yesterday. Three

Laurel

varicose veins are curled like broken tracks across skin, hardened by perseverance and the September sun.

Treacherous.

Her hair is a mass of gold and brown curls pulled back into a ponytail with an old elastic band. She wears a grey T-shirt this morning, one that does not outline the pout of her breasts. We do not speak.

I gulp down deep breaths of air, opening my lungs to a landscape that is alien. I feel defeated. It is too hot for me. I quicken my pace, move over to the left and stand under the shade of a shrivelled-up olive tree. Fields of burnt-up earth stretch out into the horizon.

'Are those melons?' I shout out. 'They look more like dried-up carcases.' I cast my hand tentatively over the skull of a green ball, the colour of silvered cucumber. I turn it over, curious and disbelieving. Its inside pulp is battered and bloodied, filled with seeds, dead flies and horse excrement.

She does not hear me, trudging ahead at a faster pace, her feet free-wheeling from right to left, dismissing the squalor of an arid earth, once golden, now strewn with plastic bags, bottles, half-buried bits of material, and the sordid left-overs of an abandoned meal.

The sun is burning my arms and I stretch the *kafia* out from under the straps of my rucksack so as to protect my shoulders from reddening. My fingers are beginning to swell.

Laurel –

What!

Stop.

DORIS COHEN

born 1918
Died October 16 2010.
A gentle and loving lady.
Who made aliyah[6] *at the age of eighty-nine.*

I clasp my mother's hand into mine and we snuggle up, watching the surf of the Mediterranean crash onto a golden sand, dimpled by the footprints of starfish and sea urchins. It is a far cry from the cold grey water of an English Channel splashing its waves onto a pebble beach, where stones, seaweed and rubble mix without discrimination onto the decaying antiquities of Brighton pier.

Doris Cohen, born during the Zeppelin air raids of the First World War, wrapped her thick mat of hair into a loop on the nape of her neck one morning, swirled round ten times in front of the mirror and, after wedding Lionel Nathanson, posed proudly but sheepishly for photographs. Bombs raged down nightly just across the water, by St. Paul's. It was November 1940. One year later, she conceived her first child, Patricia, during a British Army training mission in Cork, Ireland. Lionel had come home –

The second was conceived in Brighton. As for the others, I have utterly no idea. Metropolis of London, I should imagine.

It is 1946. One o'clock in the morning, Lewes Hospital. My mother lies in a pool of blood.

'This child will never survive,' she says. I try to prove her wrong.

55 CLISSOLD ROAD
STOKE NEWINGTON
1923

Doris's head just reached the top of the mottled marble dresser. She screwed up her nose. Her mother, Hetty, was skinning fish – live ones.

Doris remembered the slime and innards dropping onto a cold stone floor. She would mash it about with her fingers, smearing it into her hair, an immense mass of golden frizz that sprayed around her head like silken twine, each one curled and braided a hundred times over.

Doris and Hetty, her mother

SAFED

Nearly ninety years later, I gently lift the glasses off Doris's nose and place them on her bedside cabinet. I then unhook the plastic oxygen cord from the metal box standing beside her, loop it gently across the crown of her head and down towards the edge of her nose, and insert the end bits, curling upwards, into her nostrils – not too far. I don't want to hurt her. Three tiny thread veins protrude out of the left one. I've inherited the same. When she closes her eyes I notice the full width and depth of her eyelids; her wrinkles recede into the distance.

Her breathing is soft now, almost regular. I watch her stealthily. I hear the shrill, high-pitched whine of a kitten, attempting to draw on my sympathies. The wind blows into my face. It is silent, apart from the noise of rattling blinds and rustling dried-up leaves. No oaks or birches line this street. Only silver-grey bushes and jutting rocks; terraces framed by wrought iron and expensive wood, villas plastered in golds and green, radar towers on heads of hills, lookout posts from '48, black-coated gentlemen from Russian villages or LA, red-roofed bungalows, not from England.

You smile like a queen, I say to her. Then she giggles, childishly, and I stroke her cheek and kiss her and slide my lips over her neck and I know that I love her.

DORIS

either weeps or purses up her lips and speaks to no one.

Marisel, the carer, wheels the hoist into room 131 and presses her foot down onto the brake. She is methodical with her work. Strips of material have to be untangled so that they drop, vertically and undisturbed, onto the blue carpeted floor. They are hinged onto a metal bar which runs from left to right and every which way. The possibilities of how to lift a useless body onto a bed are infinite. My mother sits in the wheelchair waiting for the ultimate humiliation, to be hauled upwards by some goddamn machine which leads her not to heaven, merely to the side of a bed. She raises her arms, ready for execution, gasps for air. Her mouth gapes open. Her teeth are no longer white. Her breasts are swollen. They droop, like a pendulum, one bigger than the other.

Once I had wings.

But her voice trails off into the distance.

And howls.

Doris (left), 1930s. Still young and carefree. "Once I had wings."

PATRICIA

You think you're so posh don't you, at that fancy school.

You wanted me to go there, Dad.
You were pleased I passed the scholarship.
I thought you were proud of me.
– Patricia Har-Even

She adjusts the glasses on her nose and reads out the eulogy for mother, stands upright, straight to the point, no fuss.

Doesn't give anything away.

It is 1945 and Tricia, a blonde, curly-haired little girl is riding her red tricycle up and down the lane in front of the bungalow at Saltdean. The smell of lavender is soothing. The downs are wide and wonderful and mountains of red poppies amass on the hilltops. One day, she will run down so fast, laughing and screaming, gripping the hand of her younger sister, as they somersault, legs flying into the world of Monet.

Her mother is bending over a kitchen table, rolling out pastry. Her father grabs hold of her mother's waist. Tricia feels cross and sulky. She met him for the first time yesterday. Hates the smell of his army uniform and it's prickly. Why doesn't he go back to Italy? She scratches a scab on her knee, and it bleeds.

It is 1950. She's dragging me across Mutton Brook and racing me up the sides of old Second World War bunkers. She yells at me to come down and sweeps me up onto her shoulders to look at the weeping willow, looping a newly bobbed haircut over the bank. The trees are plentiful. Green dimpled apples hang heavily from their branches and in the distance, near an old disused tennis court, we see a red swing, swaying backwards and forwards, backwards and forwards in the wind.

We squat on mushy grass, moss and dock leaf. We splice our hands over yellow cowslip and thistle. We sluice our noses with water, so clear.

And then we see it, embedded in tiny peanuts of shingle, beside a silk of muslin draped by spiders of a thousand years, a pebble, but not just one – two and three, mottled, white, shiny glistening.

Tricia grabs the best one, hitches up her skirt and tucks it into the elastic of her school knickers. When she wants something, she gets it.

*

Why did you hate me?

I think it was because up to the age of three years and seven months I was brought up in a single parent family, no father, no sibling. Hell, I was the star of the whole show! Can you wonder at my perplexity when other people crowd into my universe where I am, as in pre-Galilean science, the planet at the centre of the system.

First, a stranger, male, an alpha male, loud and dominant, pushes in, followed only seven months later (remember you were premature) by a squalling, fat, unpredictable babe, who takes over the attention of both mother and grandmother.

Of course there are ways to obviate sibling rivalry, as we now know – gentle introductions, encouragement to hold and touch and feed, presents and gifts purportedly from the new sister. But this didn't happen, none of it did! As soon as you were born, when I was four years and two months, I was put into nursery school in Saltdean, not in the house, puzzled, and possibly a nuisance when I came home, perhaps not utterly welcome, interrupting the baby's routine.

Who knows? There is no one to ask anymore, no one to explain. It was bad and didn't get better until we were both grown women with families of our own. It has been, until the last fifteen years, a tragedy of suspicion, anger, fear and resentment. What a waste.

– Patricia Har-Even

*

And then it's 1957 and she's chasing me, and be careful, I'm going to break my head open and be careful –

Dad is lifting your skirt and slapping your thighs and why are you shoving your hand through that pane of glass and look there's blood dripping everywhere and Mum is sobbing, look what you've done to her and why do you always go out with non-Jewish boys and okay, I did hide your handbag. I was jealous you see, of the poet from Oxford, who I too wanted to kiss.

Fifty years later, Patricia pulls herself up from the floor sharply, holding her hip and complaining about her joints. She glances in the bedroom mirror, picks up a pair of tweezers and plucks a hair from her cheek.

I watch her carefully. She's been unusually affectionate today, helping me sort papers and sift through hundreds of old brown envelopes and press cuttings. All of a sudden there's a deafening bang and one of the metal storage boxes from a top shelf of her wardrobe crashes to the ground and springs wide open.

Torn letters, crumpled address books, keys, reels of cotton, stockings and odd gloves spill out onto the carpet. My grandmother's personal effects. Quite staggering. Mrs Hetty Bendel. The one and only Mrs B.

RODNEY

My only brother.
Chip off the old block.
Dropped names like nobody's business.

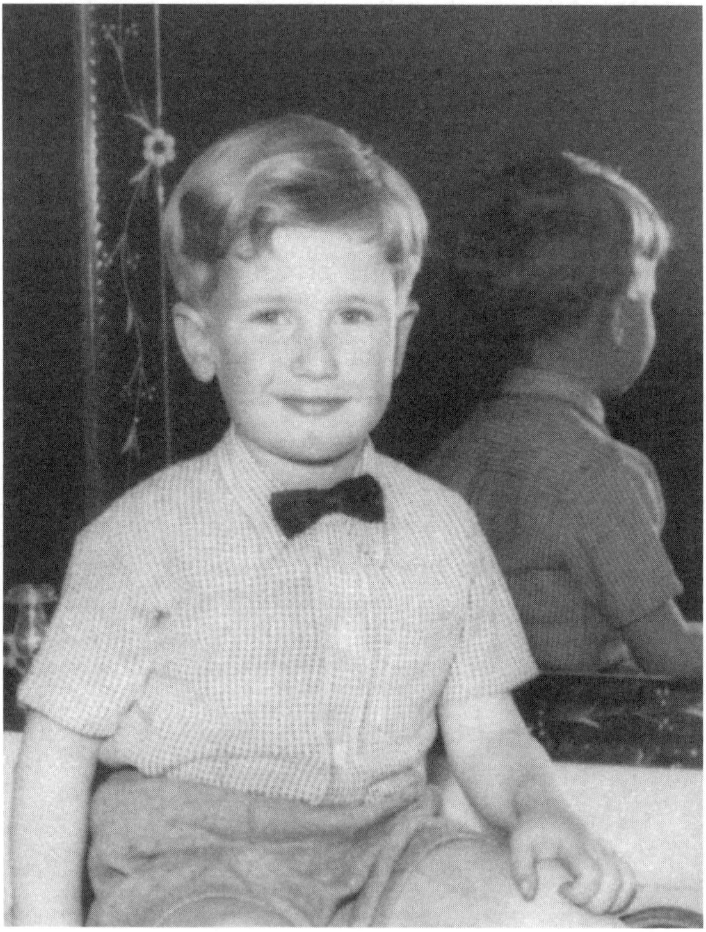

Rodney, 1953. Year of the Coronation.

The glass-fronted photograph stands on my mantelpiece. Rodney, three years old, sits there smiling and handsome, in bow tie and short jersey trousers. A lock of white-blond hair falls onto his forehead. It is 1953, the year of the Coronation. He must have stayed at home that day, looked after by a maid –

He certainly wasn't at number 49.

Tricia grabs hold of the binoculars, and stares out of the sash window of the fourth-floor flat, opposite Marble Arch. It's her turn, her turn to see a real fairy queen in shimmering jewels wave to the crowds from a golden coach. She opens her mouth wide and starts to shriek. Doris claps a hand over the child's lips. Eddie lifts Tricia up and sits her on his shoulders. His mother, Hetty, stands tall, stomach sticking out, legs astride, one hand placed on her hips, the other pinching a nostril.

That's what she did.

All the time.

Mrs B.

Sixty years later, my brother climbs down the stairs of his flat, slowly, gingerly.

How are you, Rodney?

What do you care? Can't you see your brother on a Sunday?

And as for the Sabbath.

You call this *Yom Kippur*, Day of Atonement.

Bloody atonement sister, where are you?

What would Mum be saying in her grave?
Huh.

I bang on the door with my fist. It is secured by metal shutters. I peer through the letter box and see his face. He grasps the bolt and pulls it open. He stands there, like a prison bailiff, shaking, gripping hold of two bunches of keys, dry skin peeling above his lips, plastic catheter poking out, hairy chest.

He's put on weight, jerks his knee – curls his fingers into mine and takes my hand to walk upstairs. I flick the switch down of the new, shiny Russell Hobbs kettle, turning my face away from a sink clogged up with chipped cups and saucers, plates and the remains of a Friday night dinner. I see his toenails long, irregularly shaped, filthy.

He speaks of Lily's death.
His lady friend.
Don't understand, he says.
Don't understand.
Like a foetus.
When she had her stroke.

She did care for you my love.

And now you live inside your beetle pot, and scream, all in a muddle and take a hundred steps to sit, anywhere, back and forward, up and down, yelling at me– What's going on, tell me! What the hell is going on?

Dad, your hair was slick and brylcreemed, beginning to recede. You drove a metallic car – green, I cannot forget. Mum is waving you goodbye, in her forties, trying to hide her belly from us. It's swelling. She's growing another. The one before, number three, is pushed aside, ignored, chastised, patronised, bullied, shamed and dismissed.

Is that why he stole upstairs on a summer's evening, closed the door and hid away? Is that why he fled from school, not knowing how to stand his own ground? Is that why he pussy-footed to college, mixing with girls he knew not how to answer? Is that why –

Is that why Rodney shakes?

Watch him now, dearest father. Watch him, as he stretches out to reach an orange, wedged on to a plate at the back of a fridge, to pierce it open with overgrown nail. He's hungry, dearest Father.

He's been living on tea and toast for over a week. He shovels a stale crust of bread into his mouth. He curls up into a pitiful ball.

CAROL

You have to make things happen.
That's what I've always done in life.
If you don't, you disappear.

You think anyone's going to believe you? You think you can carry on re-inventing yourself to kingdom come? Nearly sixty years old, lived a collection of lives, convinced you can keep doing this until you drop and are bent, decrepit, wrinkled, sagging from the breasts downwards – you can't hide the slow, slow disintegration.

I try to remember how it all began.

It was the lavender, thick bunches, wild and mauve, smelling as soft as the talcum powder that lay discarded and unused, defeated, on the top of Grandma's dressing table, inlaid with gold.

There was so much happiness in that old bungalow in Saltdean.

I think I was three years old then, long plaits, quarry tiled floor, Grandma kissing my cheeks, picking poppies and stomping over green baby-topped hills, as smooth and rounded as the *kneidlich*[7] she'd make on a Friday night – dropping them gently into bubbled boiling water and then wetting her hands and shaping meat loaves, moulding them, squeezing them and finally lining them up into even patterns onto old metal baking trays.

The family said that times were glamorous then. Tricia talks of fancy parties, press cuttings and Labour Party meetings.

I just remember the fourth-floor flat in Marble Arch, the grubby black railings of a cranking lift, the stale smell of burnt-out cigars, the stained toilet seat, the cocktail cabinet, walnut and decadent.

And the heaving Hoover magnanimously overseen by the weekly char. Her name was Margaret. Dear Margaret. She even invited me into her bedroom once. All her little glass jars laid out on the mantelpiece. She'd stay over on a Tuesday night to grill Grandma a lamb chop and tomato, with bright green Brussels sprouts on the side. I liked Margaret.

But those days passed and Mum, wearing a knotted scarf on her head, called me back. I didn't want to go, mind – I preferred the white open-topped buses of Saltdean, but I had to and there was Mum and Dad hitting and fighting, three children and me in the middle. They sent me to school at four and at fifteen, I ducked my head and had my first kiss. 'What's the matter with you?' he said.

At nineteen, I married the wrong man.

It was your fault, Dad, right from the beginning. I always had to chase you. I didn't know otherwise. I hear my guilt at disturbing you, my pain at causing you so much sorrow and anxiety, for still I do not please you and absolve you from life's worries. I cannot free you. I tread carefully. You, my maker, must not be disturbed. But you birthed me. I am of your seed. It is not all my fault. We're in this together.

I wait by the front window, pulling the net curtain across so that I can see the lights of his car. My hair is washed and parted in the middle. I want him to let me light the *shabbas*[8] candles and say the *bracha*[9] over the bread. I've even chopped the liver and grated a mountain of yellow bits on the top.

Always a feeling of waiting for him –

Never the other way round. Except of course when the unexpected happened.

I have cancer.
He hasn't.

I was fifty. He came to see me – a real personal visit, one to one. Not a family tea of bridge rolls and smoked salmon sandwiches. He wouldn't take a taxi, mind –

Too expensive. Got the wrong tube on the Northern Line, jumped out at Camden by mistake. Mum went home. He persevered. A dapper-looking sixty-year-old. But he wasn't sixty. Lionel Nathanson was born in 1915.

'You're eighty-one, dear Father.' He was so smart that afternoon. Brown, tweedy suit. Lost a little weight. Top of flies still undone. Beige raincoat, light brown walking stick and white Panama hat.

I never noticed his feet before. Quite small, perfectly fitted into soft leather loafers.

I could hear his voice before he opened the door. Made a grand entrance. Flirted with all the nurses behind reception. As for me, I'd even put mascara on my eyelashes.

'Wish I had a dad like that,' one of the nurses said. 'I'd like to adopt him.' He walked over to kiss me. I loved his face, his smile. It was the face that tended me when I had nose bleeds. He was the one who'd wind the damp cotton wool into little sausages, stuffing them with laughter into my bleeding nostrils. He'd hold my head over the cracked enamel sink. He carried me to bed when we returned from Italy. He gave me the map to hold, to work out routes. He held my arm when I left home.

Poor old Dad, frightened of dying and desperate to hold on. He fought at home to be master, the eldest of five children, mother from England, father from Russia, culture – put your hand in your back pocket and survive.

That's what you had to do. That was his priority. But we didn't know how to talk to each other. That was the lack, this myth of a father. Yet I loved him. I had to.

The pattern was entrenched. If you don't get what you need, pretend you like what you have.

I pick up the pale blue photograph album, its pages torn and tattered, yellowing at the edges, seeking out the only picture that I really cared about, the one of a young girl dancing with her father. He was dressed in black tie, she in shimmering orange taffeta. I had a waist in those days and two breasts. I was merely fifteen years old, innocent of life, with dusky blonde hair flicked up at the ends, my father's stubby fingers cradling me.

They brought us up to never really know what was going on. They brought us up to argue, to push and shove and cry out, split us up into tucked-up skirts with hidden pockets, plates loaded up with the best, piled high with sprouts and animal fat from a white enamel bowl, always on the side, that in the end would kill him.

Carol dancing with Father, aged 15 years. 1961.

They're my photographs.
They're not, Laurel. They belong to both of us.
They're mine!
Mine!
Get off me!
You get off me! You f... crazy. Why do you panic?
Trust me.
That was the best picture we had of Dad, Laurel.
Now it's smashed!
Beshert[10].

SYDNEY 1950
Dad dreamed too, you know

It was a story I'd told all my girlfriends, jumping up and down for warmth on the playground of Brookland Primary, trying to shelter from the freezing wind, our mouths wide open, steaming into each other like the fat-arsed horses from College Farm, just up the road from Henlys Corner. Mum always took us there to watch the cows being milked. 'Our little bit of country,' she used to say.

Dad had booked the tickets, he really had – done a deal with an old man wearing a thick grey overcoat, standing behind a stall packed high with mountains of stinking cabbages and cauliflowers at the corner of Chapel Street and Liverpool Road. 'We're goin' on the Queen Mary,' he said.

'Ten pounds, only ten bloody pounds. We're goin' to have a new life Doris. It's going to be different. Hot blazin' sun, blue skies, a new beginning. The War's over.'

And Mum would stand there trembling. Her stomach bloated with seven months of pregnancy, a scarf tied over her head and her eyes, even then, slowly sinking into fear and horror behind thick-rimmed glasses at the thought of what might happen if they actually did it. Leave her Mum, Mrs B! And what would happen if her second husband, Philip, who always said he could have bought Cape Town for a hundred pounds, died; he was much older than her. And what about the girls, Tricia and Carol? How would they feel about leaving London? And anyhow, Sydney's too big a place, too far away for us. And what if we didn't like it? How would we come back?

I think about the need to finish a story about something that could have happened, something that was a part of my dad. A bit of his excitement, a bit of him, the bit that is inside me.

'Come to Australia,' the man online said. 'Come any time.'

We'd written to each other for six months now. On the Internet. This one was called Leonard. I promise you Laurel, I pressed delete.

The best time was late Friday afternoon when Dad would come in by the back door, laden with brown paper bags bursting with vegetables – cauliflowers and onions, carrots and beetroot, parsley, potatoes, peas and swedes, emptying them out on the draining board with a smile and a joke and twinkle in his eye, Mum listening with half an ear, slightly hot and sweaty from just having fried the French potatoes, rissole style and checking the pungent chicken, roasting itself dry from inside the old oven, apron tied on waist, straight skirt down to her calves, frizzed fair hair like a mountain around her head and thick glasses denting her nose. She was quite beautiful, Mum, once, I daresay.

But the antics of Dad, even the Friday joviality, hadn't covered up the screaming bully inside his fat belly, held up by tight braces and an attempt at dignity.

He wasn't dignified, my dad, only on public days, days when the lounge doors were opened to their noisy Jewish friends, talking without taking breath.

But upstairs in the bedroom, he'd sometimes hit her, twisted her arm once when she got downstairs and they stood in the hall, yelling at each other. She, still in her blue fluffy dressing gown, crying her eyes out, wiping away the tears, trying to get me (I was only little) to understand, to sympathise. I didn't know what to do. I hated it when she talked like that.

Because I loved Dad.

And I loved Grandma, especially. I remember clasping Grandma's hand, tight, on the bottom platform, and then we sat down on the long, chequered seat nearest to the conductor. I liked his black uniform, quite posh, and that shiny metal ticket machine strapped across his chest. I wanted to keep the ticket. He pulled the handle down and it made a swishing, ringing sound. And then Grandma said I could go upstairs. The bus was white and open-topped and I sat right there in the front looking out over this enormous world of sea and frothy waves and squawking seagulls and in the distance the dark, foreboding bricks of Roedean.

'Grandma, Grandma, are we getting off now? Don't let him go. Not yet. I'm still coming down the stairs.'

I was so excited, swallowing all that fresh air

and trying to keep up with Grandma's footsteps, noticing that her shoelaces weren't tied up properly and she had thick ankles and wore a navy blue costume that fitted snugly into her waist and her bosom was quite plump and oh, she was so smart!

I didn't miss Mummy. God knows why she sent me away to Saltdean when I was three, to live with Grandma.

She was pregnant with my brother –

STRATFORD AND EAST LONDON
MUSIC FESTIVAL
1928
Doris Cohen, aged ten, presented with a medal,
inscribed with the words:
'Sing with your clear voice alone'.
She melted your heart –
Dispatched at the age of fourteen to a noisy,
cramped dress shop in Chapel Street, Islington.

I try to imagine my mother as a dancer, a singer. She wanted that.

Doris stands for a moment at the top of the banisters, and breathes deeply. She is dressed in a blue sequinned evening gown, with pearls clasped around her neck and white satin gloves on her hands. It is after midnight. She hears the heavy tread of my father's feet on the stairs. 'Ladies' night' is over.

Her head shakes.

Always shaking, agitated, nervous.

★

Grandma Bendel, Mrs B, was different, a woman of 'real substance', hanging out coats and dresses on a rail outside number 2, White Conduit St, and reminiscing about her own mother, selling lingerie to actresses in Drury Lane, from a rented barrow outside a stage door.

Now it was her turn, resolutely smiling at everyone, until good fortune came her way again and she was picked up by a polite, black-coated gentleman – a passer-by from Cape Town, Lithuanian and wealthy. First time round, she married a Pole. Not a reliable man. He said goodbye to my mother at Warren Street Station, gave her a couple of quid and sailed off to America. Oooh – Grandma had been so careless, losing her first husband to a blonde.

When Grandma told me her stories, she'd make a movement with her thumb and index finger, just the tips, and then sort of squeeze the fleshy edge of her nostrils together. Two round, black, scary holes. Mum said it was the Moldavian ancestry in us. I liked the thought of that. It gave me a feeling of belonging to something much bigger than myself.

I can hear her now. She spoke so softly, whispered –

Do you remember Leah, your great-grandmother?
I do.

I remember her sitting in the doorway of her shop, thin, gaunt, wrapped up in a long black dress. The wind was blowing hard. She was selling buttons and Alf, her eldest son, was down below, chopping herring and slicing *wursht*. He was a gentle man, fell in love with a *shiksa*[11] once. He lifted his violin off the floor, curled his fingers round the strings, plucked three times and whispered in my ear, 'Beethoven.' One night he was weary. He put his violin back into the wooden case and climbed back upstairs to bed, for good. These things happen in families –

Alf, the violinist. "He was a gentle man."

Grandma.
I will tell you my story.

Tuesday evenings, straight after school, I'd go along to *Habonim*[12]. I'd clamber onto a 102 bus and drive past all those big fancy houses in Muswell Hill, hearing the scrape of those knotted branches; trees with growths that looked like a plague of embarrassed boils, plunder into its red roof and cause the whole of the first year of Tollington to hurtle into each other's arms and throw their Juliet caps to the wind.

I was a small, curly-haired twelve-year-old, wanting to entrench myself into the bustle and vigour of the *moadon*[13] in Finchley Road; hundreds of us, wearing blue shirts, dancing, arguing, camping near Matlock and sitting on the old Esse stove in the cold stone-flagged kitchen of a Sussex farmhouse – aspiring to a 'better' life, a true socialist life, 'tilling the soil' in the hills and plains of a new Israel. We were idealistic, we sucked in the indoctrination of our 'new faith' like hungry babies.

I will tell you where I met my first man, one that didn't go off with a blonde. It was down at the Eder farm, three miles up from Dial Post, near Horsham. I was bewitched by a picture of a woman wearing a headscarf and carrying a basket of eggs. It was the beginning of my pastoral dream. I stayed with him for twenty years. He taught me to make French toast, clean a toilet and shovel up cow shit, not to mention making hay while the sun shines between the end of breakfast and the beginning of *Desert Island Discs*. Mrs Stuart would scream up the stairs, 'Where are you girl?' and I'd race down, brushing the straw off my trousers, pulling at my plaits and rushing out to help her wheel the milk churns back down to the cowshed. Her old man was probably lurking around somewhere and I didn't want to get in the way of him.

THE PROMISED LAND

1966
We took a ferry to the Promised Land –
It was the perfect metaphor for an idealisation.
The collective would heal.

If you want to marry me, Carol,
we go to kibbutz.
That's the deal.

Carol and Edward. "If you want to marry me, Carol, we go to kibbutz."

Okay.
Call me Shoshana.
Shosh.
It's my middle name.
In Hebrew –

We sailed for five days over the seas, leaving Marseille late because a tug had bashed into our ship, sleeping in cold bunks at the transit centre, covering up our noses from the stink of excrement on walls with peeling plaster, tottering from side to side on top deck and wondering if it would all be okay in the end, staring at endless, endless waves crashing into the ship's hull.

★

June 5th, 1967
Israel flew over Egypt.

Syria screamed.
For twenty years we'd dreamed of driving to Damascus.
Forget it –
The War was a disaster for the Arab world.
A future of endless chaos for Israel.
Today, still not resolved.
Conflicts sourced from the testaments of God.

AMIAD[14]

I remember Yehudit, she traipsed down to the laundry, with a bag of dirty washing. Marty pulled her elastic stockings up, plonked a tin helmet on her head and switched the machines back on. Never made a fuss, that woman.

That's when we heard the sirens.

Rosh Pinna, the next *yishuv*[15], glowed bright, bright orange on the horizon, like a ball of fire. A shell smashed through a children's house, in one side and out through the other. Dad's Army from *Hatzor* fell over each other, yelling at us to hurry up and rush to the shelters. Two of my best mates grabbed a blanket and burst into hysterical laughter. One dashed and one waddled – thirty-six weeks, she was. A middle-aged woman hid under a bed convinced that nothing would happen. Mina, my son's nursery nurse, was terrified; her husband had to go off and dig a trench. Military order.
Not to be refused.

Fear fused by trivia –

A Catholic volunteer fell out of bed, clutching hold of her rosary and saying two Hail Marys. Antoinette, known by everyone as 'Twinkle, Twinkle', shoved her polished shoes in a cardboard box and stowed them away at the back of an air raid shelter, promising her father, a high-ranking officer in the

British Army, that she refused to be a volunteer any longer, and was flying home on the next plane. It was back to finishing school and that was that –

Naturally the mini skirt was an eclectic symbol of internationalism, but when Belinda, a Glaswegian volunteer, ruined all her clothes by shrinking them in the communal laundry wash, she discovered that her one remaining mini skirt, flapping around her thighs, was not conducive to hanging off ladders against fruit trees and totally inadequate for loading supplies off trucks in the middle of the night when the temperature dropped to below freezing – or so it seemed.

As to the Danish and Dutch – they merely hugged everyone in sight and made love in an orange grove. The Beatles immortalised them. Janis Joplin made them cry.

I rush back to my room to collect a half-eaten cheesecake, hoist my arms under the strap of a rucksack, fill it with baby stuff, toothbrush and toothpaste, and dive over to the children's house.

Babies are dragged out of beds, taps left running, a two-year-old boy dribbles saliva onto his vest, clings to his mother's arms.

The dark silhouette of a cypress tree swings low over my right shoulder.

A frog is calling.

The metal door of an air raid shelter, covered in graffiti, is illuminated by a tiny flame from inside a

Tilley lamp, held up by my husband. He clutches hold of me and tells me to hurry down, lifting our child out from beneath the blankets of a huge perambulator, a relic of the forties. He pushes it open with his foot. A shaking woman cries out to her child, a coat wrapped over her nightdress.

I clamber down, tentative. I take short, sharp breaths. My son whimpers. I hold him tight to my chest. He is merely five weeks old. I am merely twenty. Shadows of muted light force me to screw up my eyes. The air is stale, like unwashed bodies that have never seen soap. Wooden boxes, coffins, lie empty upon a raised bench to the left of the shelter. I lay my son in one of them. I untie the cord of my rucksack and drag out a cot sheet and woollen blanket. I kiss him gently on his face. I tell him not to cry. I slide his box to the edge of the bench and then rock him backwards and forwards, backwards and forwards.

Tishon chamud, tishon[16].

The air-raid shelter has no toilet; plaster falls from the ceiling. Half-cooked chickens congealed in fat are stacked into a plastic box. Two or three dozen ripe avocados are thrown alongside. A young boy empties a bowl of oranges and stuffs them down his trousers. Milk sours.

A man in uniform yells at my husband to race over to the *chader ochel*[17].

My mother-in-law phones from Nottingham. She wishes us happy anniversary.

Wishes Edward and I happy wedding anniversary.

By the third day, I'd had enough; my baby needed his hair washed. A shell nose-dived into the apple orchard. Six young mums said 'sod it', jumped over three steps and disappeared into the bushes. I remember those women, driving up from *Korazim*, one of the neighbouring villages. They weren't scared, just got on with everything, checking there was sufficient water in the jerry cans, parcelling up bottles of milk, nappies, blankets and baby clothes, stuffing everything into the back of some Jeep and talking, nineteen to the dozen.

And they took over *our* shelter.

'Goldfinger' (that was the gynaecologist's name) showed Ruti, the nurse, how to cut a woman, if she delivered at an inconvenient time. 'You'll scream,' he said. 'I won't,' she told him.

Three nights running, we heard the sound of the tanks, same sound every night, moving in from the back of the kibbutz into *Wadi Amud*. There just weren't enough. We didn't have a choice. We had to attack.

That was when we heard the stories of infantry travelling in *Egged* buses to the foot of the Golan, dying before they managed to get out.

That's when people got excited.
That's why young men go to war.

I STAYED ON KIBBUTZ FOR SEVEN YEARS 1966–1973

SUMMER

The walls of Shosh's room are white, a few objects adorn the plaster that is cracked – a picture, flat basket, some bells. The floor is tiled. In the corner is an iron bed, double, with a sheet. In the middle is a door that leads onto a small balcony. It is hot and she is already wanting another shower. She sweats. At thirteen minutes past three, desire breathes onto her. Tiny slats of light enter through the narrow window. She read somewhere once that one should marry a man who can sit with a woman easily. She sighs.

Their rhythms jar. When he sleeps, she wakes.

Shosh's T-shirt is sliced off her shoulder, showing a faded white bra-strap. Trickles of sweat glisten provocatively in the crease between the breasts. She does not bother to wipe it off. For the fifth time that day she tucks her apron underneath the elastic bottoms of her shorts. She looks down at her thighs, presses her thumb into the top half of one of them and wishes it was firmer. Would it make any difference? If she was wanting –

She will finish folding a few more nappies, check to see if the babies are sleeping, wait for Naama to replace her on the afternoon shift, pick up a jug of milk on the way home, meander carelessly through eucalyptus and bougainvillea, glance wistfully at avocado trees and finally reach her destination. She will pull off misshapen leather boots, stick the socks, smelling, into the laundry bag, peer into the bedroom to see if her husband sleeps and open the fridge, feeling irritated if there are no apples. Her husband is manager of the packing shed. He should think about these things.

Shosh is tired. She is still breastfeeding her second child, a daughter, rising at five and working a full eight-hour day in the kitchen. She is only with them from four to seven, apart from feeding and bath time.

Not enough.

I want to say I'm sorry.
I remember that moment.
You walked into the kitchen.
A small, fresh smelling toddler.
Clean white pants and vest.
A small, green apron neatly tied over your tummy.
Your tiny feet grounded in safe brown leather boots,
pristine white socks folded over your baby ankles.
Your face scrubbed and shiny and your eyes large,
wondrous, blue and magnificent.
I sat you on the top of the table and kissed you all
over, making faces and laughing.

WINTER

At five a.m. Shosh rises. Her husband is gentle. His waking of her is slow.

He does try.

It is cold. She shivers, pulls a vest out of a drawer. Edward lights the paraffin stove and boils up a kettle of water. Shosh dresses herself in bed. She wears the same clothes as the ones she wore yesterday, apart from her underwear. She gulps down her tea and rushes out onto a pathway, that joins countless others.

She is breathless. The kitchen is cloaked in steam from the boilers. She ties up her hair in a headscarf and wipes her hands on her apron. Fifteen boxes of chickens to be cleaned. Lunch to be cooked for three hundred people.

Her shift is eight hours long. If she leaves early, even by one minute, Rosie will shout at her. Rosie is in charge. Everyone is afraid of Rosie, born in Glasgow, lived on Amiad for a thousand years –

Or so it seems. She knows it all. But Shosh has to admit, Rosie's pastry is amazing. It melts in your mouth. It's knowing how much butter to use. That's the trick.

★

I feel hemmed in by baskets of unsorted laundry, pans of white beans just coming to the boil, dishes unwashed and soiled dishcloths, people shouting, tensions –

Children sleeping and those awake, cats clawing at doors for milk and music, piped, from over the hills, calling Arabs to prayer. Rains came down from the heavens this morning. Water puddles on the side of paths leading nowhere. The washer and drier is stored in a narrow shed, and sand and pebbles of varying shades drown in stagnant water that grows higher and higher onto a garden deep in mud and dishevelled by the overgrown branches of a bush, whose smell takes me back to years long past. My nose is bewitched by jasmine and rosemary and I am walking fast by a children's house, torch in hand, and it is three a.m. and still four hours to go before I can sleep.

I am on night duty.

I kick the goat bucket and chuck a handful of carrots through the iron bars. I only saw my son for half an hour this morning. I wish it could have been longer.

It was meant to be our dream!
We stay here, Shosh.
No. Enough.

Four weeks before the Yom Kippur War, we go back. We'll sleep in my old bedroom, Dad. Split the mattresses.

★

Thirty years later, I return.

I heave my case onto an *Egged* bus and stare at Arab villages, buried into the sides of hills. Less than fifty yards away, families are poking the low, stunted olive trees with sticks. A grandfather tugs at a small boy's sleeve, hugs him close to his chest and pushes him back to work.

I hear the sound of the water sprinklers. The spray is fierce. Its regularity is soothing. The rhythm never changes. It is kibbutz.

I lie on my bed in the afternoon and hear the same sounds. It comforts me. I watch people, counting the number of lines on their skin, remembering their names, the smells, the colour of their clothes, the repetition, saying good morning or trying not to. Nothing changes.

I close my eyes –

Yesilka tightens the belt of his trousers, tucks in his faded blue shirt and pulls his jacket in tighter. He wants to protect his chest from the early morning cold. Yesterday he worked until sundown and missed his siesta. Thirty olive trees had their produce knocked to the ground. Geveret Brenner is already up, out on her balcony, placing a teapot and mug on a small wooden table and knocking her hip in the side of the wall. Little children creep out from under blankets and playfully open the fridge, unscrewing bottles of iodine and spilling it on the floor. Yehudit, the *metapelet*[18], will not arrive until six. Rochelle and Dvojak reach for the alarm clock and heave a sigh. They are tired and weary. It's too early to leave their beds. Ma'ayan and Mina bend their heads down to the ground and giggle and gossip unmercifully. They walk to the *chader ochel* in shorts and aprons tied behind and old leather boots, open at the ankle. Their arms are always folded. In the distance are Hebrew voices. Down in Tiberius, they are warming *pitot* and sprinkling paprika on the hummus.

It is six a.m.. The sky is yellow and dust pours out from the Sahara. Trolleys piled high with disordered clothing trundle backwards and forwards from industrial washing machines to laundry shed. Ladies sit and fold.

I remember the day I arrived. Two a.m. Mike was on night guard duty, lifting the chairs onto the tables so that the floor could be washed first thing in the morning. I had a blinding headache.

When we left, I bent low and whispered in my son's ear –
A silver aeroplane is waiting for us.

Why did you leave? people asked.
I told the same story to everyone.

I was untying my bootlaces.
Standing on the stone path in front of my room.
Just by the lemon tree.
I saw the tortoise.
Came every day.
Like everything else.
No surprises.
I couldn't stand it.

I will decide when to bury scratched fingers into clumps of earth and pull at the roots of weeds –
When to scrape my fingers around the edge of a bowl of cream –

When to walk.
When to run.
I will decide.

JOHN

Sometimes it takes years and years to see a pattern, but watch a tin of paint when it falls and spreads unmercifully across the carpet. You can't stop it. The stain just gets bigger and bigger and bigger, like secrets, passed down from generation to generation. Each family fiddles with the story, changes a fact here and there, tries to protect itself. From what –

Shame.

We have to stop it.

My room curves up high into the slated roof
of an old barn.
Built originally for the horses, now merely a place to
escape to.
I used to wonder what that meant –
Fen country.
But now I understand and I'm falling in love.
Go on, try and cut the silence, go on, slash your way
through it. You won't succeed.
Can you hear the furred rustle of the trees?
High into the sky.
White, cold, barren.
I've discovered a secret place down by the river,
where the grass is thick and mushy and the slope
bent and unashamed. I'll ride my bike over there
tomorrow. It'll be the middle of the afternoon,
when time is not sure which way to go, when cakes
are turned out of their tins and iced, and girls in
smocked dresses with wide open legs cry out for
heaven.
Funny how things turn out. But I am quite
happy like this, alone.
You are inside me, and for the time being that is
enough.

JOHN

It is time for the polar bear and the whale to talk.

BACKFIRED

Eight o'clock; dinner eaten, washing machine loaded, ironing basket stuffed back into cupboard. Shosh picks up the phone and dials. His voice is deep, solid, like Brahms.

The sun was enormous, a great ball, bright, bright orange. But then it was gone.

It left her, alone, nervous, tentative, cold, jagged and quivery. She adjusted the black crocheted shawl, and wrapped it tighter round her head and shoulders; she walked fast, gusts of air curling up from a mouth, half-open. She stared at the woman walking in front of her with greasy, unwashed hair and fag hanging from mouth, the child kicking a ball against the sidewalk and the old man sleeping on a park bench, clutching two empty beer cans.

She gazed at the ghosts of silver birch trees screaming out to stay alive and the piles of rubbish, kicked into a garden, once planted with tulips, now covered in shit –

Snowflakes splattered onto her shoulders. It was too early to knock. She stood outside on the pavement and looked up. His curtains were drawn. Front door needed a coat of paint; garden needed digging. She glanced at her watch.

Time ladies –

He had straight white hair.
It fell onto furrows of a brow.
You look frozen. Do you want a drink? Coffee or tea?
Whatever you're making.
For fuck's sake. Coffee or tea!

A dog-eared Bible lay discarded under a cushion.
The lamp was broken. She stared at John and didn't say a word.

Why are you here?
I was born.
Quickly.
Storm.
Blood.
Fell out.
Unexpected.
Mum said I'd never survive.
It always feels like that.
I say nothing and then I explode.
She rubs the tears across her face.
Oh yes.
And divorce –
Then burst into laughter.

COMFORT OR TRANSGRESSION

Shosh stands in the entrance hall, leaning back against the radiator. She hears the sounds of voices, a door being opened, a woman being ushered out. She hears someone running down the stairs; the front door is slammed.

And then she is walking up the stairs and he is standing there and looking at her and daring to brush his hand over her head and say how magnificent she looks and why hasn't she ever cut her hair before and then he comes nearer and she steps back and he asks why she does that and she says she doesn't know.

She places her hand on her stomach.

Come here woman.

I don't know what to say.

Cut the crap woman. Spit it out.

I better stop paying you. I mean things are different now –

Aren't they?

I was smitten with John's house. It was huge, spread out over three floors. Old Regency terrace just off Camden Square, where black railings with sharp iron heads faced onto unkempt lawns and piled up high moulds of brown, late autumn leaves, not the golden kind which inspired you to book a B&B near the bottom of Scafell Pike, but the type that told you, it was all downhill now.

I lived in it twice a week, mostly on Mondays and Tuesdays, arriving at five p.m. and then scurrying away at the crack of dawn the following morning.

The papers, the telephone, the hours to be filled, waiting –

She considers the mood of her greeting. Will it be cool, composed face or will she stand by the door, ready to pounce with fist and laughter? The pale blue of his sweater is reflected in the tiny sunbeam mirror, beneath the chrysanthemums, dead leaves, dry twigs, golden spectacles and tissued words of a thousand visitors knocking on the door. They knock endlessly, streams of them. His curtains are drawn. She can see the light shining through a window. The shade is broken. Soon it will be her turn and she will slide recklessly through the barrier.

I loved the smell of tobacco touching his face. Delphiniums, tulips and pink roses beside him. The dog-eared Bible under a cushion, piles of papers everywhere. Mould blossoming in the fridge, grey fur on the side of a strawberry. The unfinished writing and me, bursting, bursting to start talking.

John was in his fifties, lonely, divorced, probably the brightest man I'd ever known. A philistine and a goy.

He was one of those men who try to make your life better.

He staggered over to the sash window, peeling off the masking tape, stuffing fag after fag into the side of his mouth.

When he sank deep into his old blue armchair, smelling of fusty cigarette ends, holes stuffed with bits of newspapers and paper clips and dried-up flower stalks, and filled his pipe with tobacco, knocking the old stuff onto the small mahogany table beside him, and thumbed through the pages of his Bible, sighing deeply and reading from the Book of Job, I was happy.

John!
Dad's died –
Yes.
I –
Miss him.
In a funny kind of way.
But he never had time for us.
In the synagogue he had the time.

In a way John's story was the same as Dad's –
Filled his life with people.
The best.
Too much.
Too many.
Loved them all.
Loved me?
Saved me.
Destroyed me.

And kept me apart.

You may sleep here whenever you like, just come. We can make a fire and sit downstairs and be warmed by the flames and say nothing.

There is drizzling rain on the window. The train shuttles along, in familiar regularity. There are only greys and browns outside, mud, bricks and puddles. A rope hangs desolately down from a crane, dingy in its yellowness; not like the bright Dinky cars clattering in boxes, hoarded for eternity, crowding the sloping eves of my attic.

Could we meet halfway, I said.
I don't mind galloping over the fields.

Nights and days. They were glorious days. The light, the river, the floods, the mud; bags of onions spilling open onto floor, wood from timber yard, leaning over, waiting to be jointed.

Put some coal on the fire, woman, and shut the door.

I swept the kitchen, old pots on the falling shelf, snowdrops peeping and there wasn't an inch of space between all those bottles, papers, nails and bags – full of apples and bulbs to be planted and paint to be mixed.

I told him of my love. Surely he should honour it. He will not marry me, yet when he pants for lack of breath and stops for a while to sit by the lock and asks if I will tie up the ropes just as he's taught me, I know that he loves me.

The narrowboat that he built is the best in the land.
A life in between.

The boat lurched uncontrollably. Sharp splinters of light cracked open the sky. Shosh pushed the tiller to the left; her hand was shaking. Moses' weeds, with thick, wavy, towering heads, tangled up with willow and hawthorn, stood two feet above the water and sprouted in disarray; silver grey rock, coated with slime and emerald green moss, jutted out of muddy banks.

On her left, an old, crumbling stone house. She saw a door and then a crow, shrieking politely, spasmodically. And then the current gathered speed and the trees were cobbled and gnarled and she was transported to another land and imagined small boys hurling sticks into swirling water and fathers knocking olives off trees and she was in Paradise – not the Promised Land.

They were stuck for hours, pushing a twelve-foot pole against the bank, trying to unpin the mushy weeds from the boat's helm.

It was pitch black when they crawled into the sleeping bag. John was embarrassed. He was utterly exhausted. He'd caught five barbel that day and thrown them back into the water. Shosh had steered – an afternoon of endless time, the water, smooth and translucent, lapping graciously. No locks for another mile. At four o'clock John had shown her how to tie up the ropes, grimacing as he tugged, his chest swelling in and out, like a pregnant rhinoceros.

She'd held him all night, his firm back squashing her breasts and the heel of his left foot pressing onto the toes of her right one.

Now she wrapped herself in her warmest fleece and pulled a deep blue knitted hat down over her head.

Five a.m.

The first blush of light seeps in through a porthole.

A stiff breeze plunders the silence
A fork slides off the table

The mist is down

In the middle of the night we'd load the car with bags of apples and bananas, potatoes and carrots and drive to a far-off land that I'd never seen.

They call it Fen Country, sweetheart.
No other place like it in the world.

The mattress was filled with horsehair and I could hear rats scuttling fast in the thatch above my head. The small leaded window, always open at night, opened onto fields that stretched a million miles away. He tells me all the time that he wants to die.

Sometimes the moon would wane and there was no time; sometimes I saw it in his eyes, sharp blue and piercing under skin that folded into tiny creases of varying lengths. I would run my fingernail along, round and inside the furrows. He was getting old now. That's how it was.

★

The seed heads of the corn brushed along the small of my back. I arched it higher, my eyes, half-closed, squinted along the sharp line of a horizon, yellow with age, and then up into a cobalt ripless sky.

John scratched a thread of hair inside the nape of my neck. The skin on his hand roughened with the years of handling old timbers.

The midges were out and it was hot. My shorts felt tight and uncomfortable, creasing their way up into the tops of my thighs and into my crotch. The seat on the bicycle was hard, it chafed my bottom. I tried to lean forward, snatching a glance through the hedgerows, sniffing the honeysuckle and noticing at the same time a slight swelling underneath my breasts. They seemed much fuller these days –

What are you doing?
It's hot.
We don't need a duvet.
John!
What are you doing now!

Let me hold you.
No.
What's this?
What's what?
Lift your arm up.
There – look!
Get off me.
God knows why I'm in your bed this morning.
Be careful – don't touch it.

OUR SECRET

Just like the cancer gnawing my inside, silent, hidden. Malignancy is a strange phenomenon. Cells grow and multiply like rats. If neglected, they turn, like people.

You'll hand me in one day.
You know the rules.
That was the blackmail.
We were hooked.
I wasn't afraid of the war in '67.
I was afraid of this.

★

Nothing to worry about – the consultant said.
Probably benign.

He jabbed the needle in. Nothing. Sent me for an ultrasound. Took it out the following week. The truth is I quite enjoyed the drama. It was like being in a play. I remember locking the front door. It was a nice day. I felt quite excited. I thought, I must prune the passion flower. I didn't really want the lead but if I got it, I'd manage, I mean, if it was malignant –

When the fantasy starts to take over, you realise how little you're in control of whether you live or die.

'It's your choice,' said the consultant. 'Cut or treat?'

'We didn't see it on the mammogram. Terribly sorry, we're really sorry. Suggest we dig in, take some stuff out, sew you up and give you a dose of radiation. Of course, if you prefer we could just take it off altogether. The left one, that is.'

So I agreed to have another operation. Axillary clearance. Breast was healing, still sore and swollen. Very common. They say it leaves a small dent.

Told me I had to wait.

'The news is good,' the consultant said. 'One of the lymph nodes was cancerous, but that's in the dustbin now. There's no evidence of cancer having spread any further. A bit of pre-cancerous tissue around, but I'm sure we can sort that out with the follow-up.'

Funny how things work out.

Dad.

Before he died.

The two of us.

The same.

Doctor, will you get me out of here?
The nurses have all gone home.

Are you serious? I can't eat for ten days? You're on a drip. You keep vomiting. Your blood is poisoned. What more do you want? You've also got mouth sores – down below as well.

Can I get up to use the toilet?

No, you've got a commode.

When I shout to have it emptied, nobody comes.
We're busy.
Are there any nurses?
No.
None.
No.
You're short-staffed.
Short-staffed.

⋆

Having breast cancer isn't just about being afraid to die. It's about wanting to live in the fast lane. You still want him to go down on you, and if he does find a lump –
Wherever –
It's like shooting a hole in one at the local golf course.
You know that I joke.
I have to.

My heart was slow this grey, still, flat morning of promise. I moved with slow steps, my leg filled to the brim with water or so it seemed. It ached. It was heavy and allowed me no relief. A reminder of the passing of time, slipping indiscriminately away from myself and nearer into the humdrum domesticality of a tedium of days with no difference. What had I learnt from time? To ignore it, to just notice the change of light at the crack of dawn. To try to forget.

The doctor smiles politely at me but doesn't really listen. 'Everyone tries to write a story about cancer. There's nothing original to say. Anyhow, I'm not the right man to ask.' His face is older now. There are more lines, creases, he looks quite tired. But why doesn't he really ask me how I am? Because he can't. Because he knows that both of us just carry on, that life is a treadmill and there's no difference. We are the same.

Whatever the force inside me is to stay alive. I am not scared. I just feel utter despair and hopelessness when I get the pain. He tells me I *am* doing well. I am doing well –

I'm sick, sick, sick of this grey dismal life, of this cancer life, of a cell that scratches the surface of my bowels, of a leg that swells below the knee, of a vagina that has forgotten – touch, of a stomach that is expanding, of an isolation that kills me, of trains that are nothing more than wagons, carrying the dead to their fate.
I am reminded.
Did they know?
As I do.

I must not cry because if I cry the cancer might come back so I must hold in the cry –
So help me God. I cannot do it. I *cannot do it!*

I have repeated my stories over and over again, but you have to understand, I am confused. I know that I wake every morning and sleep at night. But when did it happen that this thing entered my body and changed the shape of me? The essence of me.

JOHN LOOKED AFTER ME

First morning after chemo, six bottles of tablets to open, all laid out on the breakfast tray. My stomach was heaving, rushed to the toilet, telephoned every doctor in the country, then I vomited.

He stayed over that weekend. I clutched onto the sheets. He dragged them off. Picked his sweater off the floor and pulled it over his head. Opened the cupboard and found my bra, threw me a pair of pants, asked me where my jeans were, pushed me out of the door, held my hand. Then we walked down to the water.

It was hot. I went home to put a pair of shorts on. John waited. We walked along the towpath, not together. He kept panting.

God.

I love you, woman. But you're all the same. You all just want a meal ticket –

And a house.

I AM THROWING THEM IN THE BIN

Give me the blue sky.
I don't care anymore. I am *not* taking tamoxifen.
Your cancer marker CA-153 is slightly raised.
I have taken it for eighteen days, and now I am
disintegrating.
From top to bottom, and as for sex –
Hopeless.
I've had enough.
I'm stopping.
F – ing pills.

★

A memory of cancer.
My mouth is shut tight. I say nothing –

He was a short man but with a straight back and handsome face. His eyes were Indian. I thought of the shamans. This man would look after me. He tells me to undress – the top half that is. A nurse (not always) sits at the side. So you lie there on the couch waiting and then he comes over and puts his hand on your breasts, one at a time, underneath, at the sides, lifting them, folding them, feeling them and the skin on his hands is soft, cool and you realise you like it. But that is not the reason for his touching. His brief is to check out for cancer. Eroticism is not the order of the day. After all it is only 2:15 in the afternoon and he is probably married and he probably looks at the top half of a woman's body as often as he has dinner. I suppose if he does find a lump, it must be quite exciting. So you try to look deadpan, as if you don't feel a thing. And you block out the thought that if you lose a breast, one, two –

No man is going to look at them again.

Ever.

CHECK UP NUMBER 11

My shaman has retired. I see a new doctor now. Every year a check-up. Mary, the Irish nurse, is still there. She's straightened her hair and looks bonny. But I miss Santalai.

'What about my hands,' I said to my shaman. And he turns them over, fingering, looking and smiles. 'Ashkenazi skin,' he says. 'Sephardi is better. We're the originals.'
He was the magic one.

My authorization number is 2314267. My name is Shosh. I know this hospital. I was here eleven years ago. Do not give me that look of bored patience and patronising condescension. You, nurse Mary from Ireland, from Belfast, who sits politely on chair beside me. Who tells me what to take off and where to put bits and hears patients, year in, year out.

Each time they come in, their faces, older and more crinkled. For some, the story has perished. For others, if lucky, the hair grows back in thin, wispy strands, parted neatly to cover the balding spot. But to me, he says, fingering a strand looped around my ear, 'Your hair is good' and I swell with pride and want to hold him. I want to say quite normal things as he touches my breasts and lifts them from side to side and feels in armpits for lumps.

And my mouth is nearly open so wide you

can see my feet and voiceless sounds erupt from memory and I want to cry. I want to cry so very very loud that even Mary, bloody Mary, will know that I am overwhelmed.

★

Fagging was a fully established system in the sixteenth century.
In Camden Square it was prolific.

I pulled open the drawer and took out a roll of bin liners. I picked up a brush and with one quick swoop got rid of it all; drawing pins, fuses, blunt pencils, bits of wire pins, staples and dried-up tangerine skin. This was my world, my secret world. It was only me who could decide what to leave on top of his desk and what to throw away, its green buff leather caked with dust, covered from one end to the other with piles of papers, half-finished stories from aspiring writers, chewed-up pencils, unopened envelopes with WC1 postmarks and unfinished sketches, done in charcoal, from some of his patients and supervisees.

John knew his work was ending. Every day from Monday to Friday he tapped his pipe onto a small table, opened a tin of Woodbine, and slowly, slowly, disappeared.

When the fascination with their games goes, when their crazy self-cripplings, conjured from infantile fantasies of uncaring mothers and weak fathers cease to engage, you are left with only boredom or saviourism.

It must have been late October, drizzly rain, squelchy pavements. I turned the telly on, watched the news. Decided to phone. I'd cleaned the whole bloody house from top to toe, heaving the Hoover up three flights of stairs, emptying waste-paper baskets, scrubbing the yellowy stained enamel bath, using innumerable bottles of Jif to get grease off walls, and changing sheets on the futon.

The phone rang and rang and rang. I tore the plastic gloves off, grabbed a fleece, stuffed keys into my pocket and drove, snatching my breath, steering haphazardly; Baldock, Royston, forget Cambridge, turn right at the inn, head for St Ives, the River Ouse. It was foggy, I turned the windscreen wipers on. I couldn't see. What on earth was I doing?

John was crouched down in front of the fire, tearing up old newspaper, stoking the coals. He didn't expect me, didn't want me. I heard this noise. Not sure where it came from – back of his throat? He was angry about something. I still had my gloves on. I drove home, shaking.

He had this rage, just like my father.

To hell with you all.
You think I'm going to be like that woman in the home.

Who whispered from a lost voice.
They kept me alive.
But I can't swallow.

I ask myself over and over again.
Why did I stay with John?

He saved my life. He found the lump. But a man too caught up in other people's lives never quite sees you.

It was a real mess. I was trapped, the prologue to his death in front of me. He'd lie there in his sleep working it all out, pulling the blankets across, burying himself down like a puppy. I'd lie there freezing, too frightened to move. Then I'd bury myself under the duvet, curling it up around my ears. A gust of cold shot in from under the cracked ledge of the sash window. That's what happens when you don't replace things. They disintegrate. I'd always found it hard to replace John.

It shouldn't have happened. I lost therapy. But the love was genuine.

Humans can mend and restore pretty well everything but themselves.

If I walked away, I'd lose him. The point is, you always think it will get better. You live with the fantasy. So you go back for more. The cycle is never-ending. To survive you have to cut.

I always remember the first time he read to me – from Steinbeck. The session had finished. I lay on the couch, a thin blanket covered my denim dress.

One night we made a snowman. I called it my 'owl and pussycat' night. The snow was dreamy. A blanket of sensuous folding. The sky was pink. The cathedral, cold and strict. We jumped and fooled around and shoved our fingers into ice and bit by bit, and slowly, slowly, our snowman grew, up and up and higher and higher. We gave him a hat and stuck an old stick inside his mouth. I laughed and brushed a fleck of snow from my cheek.

In those days the sky was blue and England was golden. Sometimes I'd joke and say, 'Let's go to Australia, for after all, how strange this world is, one side in front of the sun and the other behind.'

And then I'd leave him and go off, always hoping that this time it would be for good.

But it never was.

You can't cure old age.
You can't convert that decline into a life worth saving.

He grabbed me by the waist and pulled me to him. We stood in silence, watching the heron. And then we climbed back up onto the bridge. John unlocked the door of the Citroen, turned the ignition on, pressed his foot on the gas, waved me a desultory goodbye and drove off.

That was the last I ever saw of him.

THE TWO JEWISH BOYS

I look back on the two Jewish stories.
An unconscious belonging.

THE KADDISH

Once upon a time, many years ago,
there was a certain man who prayed in the
synagogue every day and recited the *Kaddish*[19].
'Why do you say *Kaddish* every day?' people asked
him. 'You're only supposed to say it on the anniversary of your parents' deaths – when you have
yahrzeit[20] for your mother or father.'
'But there are souls haunting the synagogue,'
he replied, 'waiting for someone to say *Kaddish* –
not merely for his mother or father, but just to
say it. I say *Kaddish* so that these souls will find a
place in paradise.'

– *Told by Hinda Sheinferber to Hadavah Sela*.
Folktales of the Jews. Vol. 2:
Tales from Eastern Europe

BENNY
A true knight.

Bitter.
No.
Realistic.
It shouldn't have happened.
Dear, sweet Benny.
Seduced me into *yiddishkeit*[21]
abandoned ship
and
fell for God.

This is the story.

TO BENNY

The pathos is that without difference, we inhabit a bland and dried-up, colourless world, that has no heritage, no identity, no uniqueness and no belief.

My name is Shoshana.
Mine is Benyamin.
Benyamin Ha Nissim HaCohen.

I'm spinning down the aisle between the golden honeyed ice creams and diamond-studded lemon sorbets and he's wearing that baseball cap that makes me want to crack up with love.

And his body is ensconced in the most delectable pale green cotton shirt, the kind you just want to unbutton, because already you're wantin', proud that it's only the two of you ziggin' around by the frozen peas because *no one else – no one*, knows how it feels at this precise molecule of a second, pinpricked into a Monday evening in Tesco's, that where you are, joined in a lush waterfall union of God and poetry and exhilaration and laughter, is a moment that might never be again.

This time the Jews have gone too far.
Too extreme.
Their *Torah*[22] will crucify us.

Benny –
It's too strict.
The matrimonial laws.
Shosh –
Understand it.

And he (the Kohen) should not marry a woman who has been divorced by her husband.
– Vayikra 21.7[23]

Shosh.
Yes, Benny?
I can't marry you. You have to be a widow or single.
In orthodox terms, you're unclean.
Huh! Clean enough for you to text me, before
shabbas[24] has gone out.

So how is the widow, Benny?
I'm not sure.
She's inhibited.
It's difficult.
Perhaps with time.
She's not like you.
I miss you.
I know – I miss you too.
Goodnight, babe.
Goodnight.

But you claim to be a religious man, Benny.
Following the laws of the patriarchal priesthood.
The story of Siddhartha comes to mind.
You yearn to cross the river –
Benny was a *chazzen*[25].
Committed adultery when married.
The *Beth Din*[26] destroyed him. They watch you all the time.
The *Beth Din* –
from the *Shtibl*[27].

Yes.

I fell in love with that one. Unavailable. Like my dad. You know how it is. We'd been out together. He'd listen to my story. But he kept on changing his mind. Three steps forward, two back. A chessboard of sin and atonement. I told him, I said – it's the unobtainable that drives the passion in your life. You do what suits you. You bury your head underneath your *tallit*[28]. You claim to be a disciple of the Levites, a Cohen of the highest order. You fondle me when I'm willing – and anyhow, I'm divorced. Forget it. And by our lot, I'm still married. Golders Green will cut me Benny –
Cut me.

But I kept bloody well going back, didn't I?
That's what's so uncanny. I suppose I wanted to be part of a family again. Belonging, tradition –
You know, all that kind of stuff.

Shosh.
Keep it a secret.
No.

PHONE ME BENNY
Why haven't I heard from you?

And then we would be together and then he would disappear and then I would ring and then he would ring but I can't marry you because I'm a Cohen but who's talking about marriage, I say, we've only known each other for a few days and then I'm rubbing my fingers across the wet of my eyes and shaking and I'm crying and I'm angry and he says something like he'll come and pick me up and I've dressed in turquoise and the sun is shining and it's Sunday afternoon when couples go out in their finery and lift up their crinolines from the mud and the skin on his face is unshaved and he looks so ravishing that I look away, lest he see the blush on my cheek and we drink cider and he, a religious Jew, pees in the hedgerow and we're laughing and I love it and I want a thousand Sunday afternoons to be like this and I'm quivering and he doesn't want me to wet my fingers with oil because when he strokes the crevices and mountain sides, he says that I am wet enough but does not want to come and bite – because he is not ready.

I remember looking at Benny for the first time. He was at least six feet tall with a sway on the hips that melted me, a face roughened with a two-day stubble, classic in its Polishness and lips that only Renoir could have drawn. I saw Odessa and Bucharest, Poland and the Pale. I liked his smile and his eyes were warm, curious. Taking in every bit of me, noting my shape.

Taxis, Westway, a quick spontaneous move. The chessboard lies open across a length of sky, optimistic in its geography. It's still south of the Watford Gap.

I see his face, rushing in with paper bags of food.

Is this woman ever going to cook for me, he thinks.

I found it amazing to be out with a man wearing a skullcap. What would my friends say? I leant back, content, resting my handbag neatly on my lap. I loved his banter. He was wearing a blue shirt. I always remember that. I considered him good-looking in a Jewish, Eastern European way, noticed a slight astigmatism in his left eye, but didn't care and that his fingers were long and pale, as if destined to plunge down on *booba*'s piano, still standing in the graveyard balconies of a Berliner world.

Our first date was crazy – jumping in a taxi to Euston, spending money I didn't have and feeling that I was whizzing high on ice cream soda. Pushy guy –
Aren't you going to allow me in?
He said.

Every morning I watched him – fist on forehead. It is the place where they think of God. It is the place to disembark and disengage, to steep deep into the past. And as he spreads his seed into the holes of woman, he heaves up in glory with something that has no words, no language. Yet the smell of it lingers in his Jewish throat and he yearns for a freedom that his diaspora cannot give. And he is torn, split, ravaged in between. Widows might be old and cracked. Widows yellow and turned to seed, virgin spinsters hard to please. His father is in the next room.

Tradition.

AND THOUGH BENNY, THE COHEN, SEARCHES FOR A WIDOW

And Shosh for a man to love and be loved by for ever.
And though they inhabit different worlds.
At this moment.
She would say.
To him.

Yes, I do.

He tells me he's coming at eleven but then there's a Bentley to pick up in Bristol and a Volvo in Malaga, a sister in Edgware who needs help with shopping and a son who's losing money. He has to visit the grounds to pay respect to Mum and Dad and anyhow the phone might ring in the middle and take him to Manchester and by the way, 'Do you know if there's a Matalan near you? I need some braces. My trousers are falling down.'

Does he really expect me to wear a blouse with sleeves dropping down to my ankles? Well, that's how it feels! I'll slip over my neck a long strand of pearls – used to belong to Grandma. I miss her.

I'm learning to be still with him but tonight I'm like a pestering dog –

I crease up when he phones during the day and tells me to hang on and he's moving a car and we're in New

York, cruising down 47th Street.

I love to see him get excited, rebel.
He always needed that. I know it.

And then he scoops me up, touching and lips gently teasing and if I wasn't falling into exhaustion, we would watch our bodies cascade into a whirlpool of skin that was hot and saturating. Then he'd push my head back, pressing his lips hard on mine, nuzzling them – murmuring sweet nothings in my ear, a surprise, always a surprise.

I HAD A DREAM LAST NIGHT

I stood with the soldiers on the coastal road, not far from the high, tumbling cliffs of Dover. Waves crashed down onto a wet, stony beach, each rock a myriad of shades of colour from dark and light greys through to flashing gleams of reds, oranges and amber.

The men huddled together in their army uniforms, cold and miserable, frightened, desperate. I knew that if I crossed over to the other side, its shape and texture now unknown to me, I would be shot at. I peered into their faces and tried to beg them to walk away.

High up above them, just behind the corner of my eye, I could see another road winding along, clear of army lorries and trucks, tanks, builders. I would go up there, I thought. I would not stay any longer.

Benny is like the soldiers – anxious. His mother's family went to the gas chambers. His father searched in books for answers and made sense of life by mending bodies. If they believed in the divine power of God's authority, penitence and faith would see them through.

Benny wakes me from my dream, stroking my arms gently. He stands by the bed, vest pulled tight over strong shoulders, *siddur*[29] in hand, *tsitsis*[30] strapped across his chest and *tefillin*[31] on his head and I want to bury my head inside his prayer shawl, black, white and billowing. I want to stand with him and pray –

And you want me to go back to the Promised Land, Benny! Why? What've Adam and Eve got to do with it, I say and turn over and run to the bathroom. He wasn't going to persuade me to join them. Yes – I remember.

The synagogue overflow.
The wheel of life.
The pulsating rhythm of the divine.
The yearly Day of Atonement.

Hold on to your knitted cap, Carol. It's *Yom Kippur*[32]. Do not slip on the floor. It's shiny, Art Deco, kiosk on either side, selling ice cream to eat, between *Kaddish* and *Amidah*[33], opposite the bus stop. You know – Temple Fortune Odeon.

Concrete steps round the back, lobby draughty, back stairs leading to the gods, hippodrome or synagogue, Golders Green, no – this is *shul*[34]. Full of children, cards and Ascot hats. But I was only eleven, red angora hat clipped to the back of my head, new woollen suit, fitted jacket, plush lining, stockings held up by elastic garters, fidgeting. Mrs Horovitch is peeping through the net and me, waiting for my father, for he is handsome and after folding *tallit*, saying *gut yomtov*[35], will grip my hand, not let me fall and my shoes are Startrite, buckled and shiny red.

⋆

I cross over to the other side of the street. The synagogue stands in front of me, devoid of beauty, lofty in stature. A light drizzle has fallen, washing and dusting the air with an autumnal sweetness that pleases me. I glance back at my car. It looks shabby with an old bicycle rack fixed to the back with heavy strapping.

Out of place.
Like me.
It is the evening of *Tisha B'Av*[36].

The synagogue hall is lined with chairs. Ladies wear cardigans and pleated skirts. Everyone's feet ensconced in plimsolls. The men are unshaven, bottles of water and plastic cups stashed away behind a heap of dustbin liners on the side of a trestle table. Benny sits in the row in front of me. I catch a glimpse of the stubble on the side of his cheek. I want to brush my hand over it. He turns his face round to check if I'm still here, then picks up his plastic bag, containing *siddur* and *tallit* and rushes out.

Nothing is ever going to change.
We inhabit different worlds.

THUS DO I SET FREE

Release thee and put thee aside, in order that thou may have permission and the authority over thy self to go and marry any man thou may desire.
Except a Cohen.

So I went to the matchmaker.
Mrs Vandecil.
Delightful lady.
Get a *get*[37]
she said.
The secret of all future happiness.
Out with the past.
In with the new.
Though you still can't marry a Cohen!
she said.
I know.
Meshugge[38] really.

I found the number in Yellow Pages – phoned them straight away. Quickly, impetuously, the fairy castle of the Orthodox, the *Beth Din*, the glorified law court of God, the place where ritual takes precedence over rationality and where woman, if divorce be the subject, bows her head to man and thanks him for letting her go. It's called a *get*. He, if he consents, has to give it to her.

A man takes a wife and possesses her. If she fails to please him because he finds something obnoxious about her, he writes her a bill of divorcement, hands it to her, and sends her away from his house[39]

– Deuteronomy 24:1

★

I open my hands, palms upward.
It flutters into my hands, like the wings
of a butterfly.
It is my *get*
to freedom –

IT WAS IN THE MONTH OF NISSAN THAT THEY MET BETWEEN SUNSET AND SUNDOWN

My name is Shosh.
My name is Maurice.
No kiddin'.
And I'm plotzing in my pants.
And blow me down we went to the same school.
He jumped on a bus to India.
And I took a boat to Israel.
How many wives?
A few.
How many men?
I've stopped countin'.
Fancy a date?

*

Midst the soft breezes of a late Indian summer, we discover a long, wild garden, overgrown with bush, thorn and rose. To my left, in a gap between two hedges, is another garden, whittled away by nettle, prickly loganberry, compost and dandelion. To my right, three dried-up flower beds filtering out to broken stile and gentle fields. Not a sound can be heard, only the tread of my shoes, meandering through thicket and bush, beech trees and pine in a landscape that is called Shropshire.

The cows sit in peace. One small, pretty calf, saturated with mother's milk, frisks her tail and jolts away. I thought about the day before, kissing Maurice with love and care, stroking his tummy and washing the collar of his shirt, sorting his socks and underwear and laying my head in his lap, reading the prayers and tracing fingernails over old Hebrew letters.

I remembered the morning after.

I squinted with delight and wiped away the sleep from my eyes. It was my birthday. Maurice stood there, half-dressed and beaming, his damp feet covered with bits of soft grass, mud and shingle, his hands holding a lemonade bottle of garden flowers, fudged up into a country bouquet.

STAMFORD HILL

Shosh, thou shalt kindle no fire throughout your settlements
on the Sabbath day!

Maurice, stop it. I'm driving over.
You're driving!
Yes.
What time will you get here?
I don't know – Whenever I fancy.
Shosh, listen to me. *Shabbas* comes in at four o'clock.
Okay, okay.
And listen, park in Cranwich Road. I'll tell Moishele
to expect you.

Thin as a rail, he was, cycling down the hill,
drooping side locks, gabardine coat and laced-up
shoes. I wanted to feed him –

A young married girl burst into a shop, grasping her
credit card, gabbling in Yiddish, theirs is a world to
which I try and belong.

Maurice, it is evening now. Look, there is a new
moon.
But he did not see it, for the clouds were grey,
moving, dank, dreary and obscure.

Maurice, my dress is velvet, soft and gorgeous,
petrol blue.
It will drape low over my legs.

I stare at the man in front of me, silk stockings, satin
dressing gown, ringlets and brimmed hat. For one
split second, I want his life, orderly, ritualistic.

It is not the custom to ring the bell. The door is left open, for any stranger, you understand. Naomi wears a wig. It is a foreign land. Shmuelik, who is angular and disjointed, is quite happy in his wheelchair, and their other five children and twenty-eight grandchildren are all part of a story, a story given to me on plates of velvet, one for milk and one for meat, one for man and one for woman, red cabbage and stewed apple and liver chopped with onion, dumplings moulded of cool white fluff and 'I shop on Wednesday, pluck on Thursday and cook on Friday.'

'What day do you make love?'
I ask.

I hear a knock on the door. Mr Grossman shuffles in, feet frozen, cannot walk. A friend follows; wears a lop-sided suit and yellow polka-dotted tie, face bent and broken, jaw stuck inside the evening prayer. The *Kaddish* of all humanity.

Maurice, let's go to a wedding.
A wedding! *Noch*. Why?
I want to see how they do it.

Maurice, look at Mr Humpeldink, stuffing bread into his mouth, and as to Mrs Weinberger, well –

What can I say.

Mrs Weinberger picks her stick up, places her hand on her bottom, massages her hip and saunters over to inspect the cakes, lifting the cellophane up and popping a chocolate cream profiterole into her mouth. Teenage girls, playing with their necklaces and twisting the ribbons around their ringlets, mill around in the entrance hall, snapping pictures, ten to the dozen –

They all giggle.

The bride stands alone in a corner, solitary. A veil hangs low over her forehead. She bends forward, cupping a prayer book in both hands, her fingernails polished with French manicure, her curls scraped into a bun, her lips barely moving as the recitation builds to a crescendo, and then you see her swaying, back and forth, back and forth, eyelids closed, expression, trance-like.

And then the crowd surges forward like a swarm of pigeons and everyone is standing on their tiptoes, trying to see and she flicks a fly from beneath her nose and holds her breath in receipt of, ooh – so many blessings, one after the other and the glass shatters into a hundred pieces and bride and bridegroom drink from the same cup.

At four a.m. before the screech of a flapping swallow, she will open her legs and check for blood. Then she will rise, drag the sheet from the bed and take it to the rabbi.

As to the men, in separate abode, they eat, stuffing their faces with eastern mezze, falafel, olives, pickles and cucumber, herring, hummus, eggs and aubergine; they dance, holding hands in an endless moving circle, sometimes faster, sometimes slower, but never stopping, changing partners, clapping hands, lifting bridegroom, sweating, shrieking, jumping, high, high and even higher, up and down, up and down.

He has never touched a girl – before.

And as to the women, they are apart, behind the *Mechitzah*[40].

Again, Mrs Weinberger, discretion thrown to the wind, creeps over to the barrier and peeps through. If she has *mazal*[41] she'll glimpse a grandson or two, three or four, five or six, ten or eleven.

The clock strikes twelve.

Maurice saunters over to talk to Mr Rechtsberger. Suzi Goldenstein gobbles up another piece of cake. Lily Lewinstein is more restrictive. Esther raves on and on about the glories of West Cliff pier – 'It's the best pier in England for *davenning*[42] on,' she says, 'wonderful – you can get away from everyone!' The newlyweds dance the *Mitzva Tanz*[43].

Maurice rubs his eyes, clasps his hands over his stomach and goes home to bed.
I fall asleep on the sofa.

Sunday morning – two days before the *seder*[44]. I rush

to buy kosher wine and almonds for the *charoseth*[45]. Three *Chassidim*[46] dash into the grocers and stare with confused eyes at the cheese counter; their legs are shapely. They will trot home with blue plastic shopping bags swinging from their wrists and peep into a kitchen to watch a woman clearing out cupboards and lining the shelves with fresh paper.

And then I flop back into my car and I'm out of it and I know that the two worlds can never be joined up. I jump from one to the other. I am in between –

My closest relationship to God is when I'm whizzing down a mountain on my bicycle –

It is inexplicable.

Shosh, what are we going to do with you?
I don't know, Maurice, I don't know –

Maurice.
Yes Shosh?
Do you believe in the *Torah*?
I do.
Does it matter who wrote it – it's extraordinary.
But Shosh, there is mystery behind the '*extraordinaire*'.

Our thoughts are the seed of everything that happens. All goes wrong when we lose control of our thoughts. It is our reaction to circumstances that prevents us seeing that we have the capacity to change them. Our thoughts are the seed of our future, the egg that gives birth to the chicken of our life.

Maurice.

Yes Shosh?

When I see the shepherd on the hills, he needs no book and is a happy man. When others observe him, they are healed, as they yearn to be like him. He needs no cult to join. He is both chicken and the egg. He is a free man.

So find your shepherd Shosh.

I will Maurice, I will.

I conjured up an image of community.
There they all were, jostling and hustling, backwards and forwards
in a crooked street, with a crooked house
with the fiddler playing.
But then I would need to escape.

WHAT BRINGS WHITE MEN OVER THE SEA

Shosh tightens the laces on her trainers and runs down to the canal, breathing heavily and scrambling over a gravelled path; a gust of wind whacks her in the face and only the hum of traffic, far, far away disturbs her equilibrium. Painted narrow boats cut through a waterway that is split into two and she bends down to slip her fingers into its glassy surface – just the tips. A tree spreads its wings beneath a mirror of rippled water. It is smooth, translucent, and she stands like the heron, alone, on the edge, jutting its long, sharp pointed beak, into a world that faces south.

The very nature of her being aches for a tension – a scrunching-up of muscles inside her stomach, a rush to the telephone to book the tickets, to fly high, high into the air and land on the edge of another country, another place, six thousand miles away.

★

Dad was a traveller, or so I imagined him. Yet, for old man Bendel, it was real – I longed to understand his world, to glimpse it, to ponder on his adventures, to make some of them my own –

DEPART HEATHROW 19:10
ARRIVE SOUTH AFRICA
11:35
20/21 SEPTEMBER 2012

My legs are squashed. Wish I was flying business class. Fall in love with the man next to me, indulging in a long haul to see his family in South Africa on the way to Washington DC. He was born in the same village as Mandela. He zips open a black leather writing case and draws Africa for me on the palm of my hand. His voice has a deep drawl. His parents had been missionaries. Heaves a big sigh. His face is chubby and he knows everything about the world. He touches my shoulder and says I can lay my head down on his lap.
Go to sleep now.
You'll wake up in Africa.
We fly low beneath the clouds and there it is, stretched out below me, the plains, the gold mines, the shimmering blue – I am skydiving into another world.

On arrival, six black women with enormous breasts open their mouths wide and sing the *Nhosi Sikelei* in welcome on the tarmac beside the plane, their voices rising up and down in separate harmonies and I am scooting back to gaze at them, before rushing to the carousel, grabbing my bags, jumping two at a time up the escalator, rucksack joggling on my back, suitcase bashing into children and grannies, and I bend my head down and shout – *Praise to the Lord!*

Are you Graham?
Yep.

Shosh or Carol! Who is it to be?
The first one.
Whatever you say, ma'am.

His ruddy orange face beams as he doffs his cap and stuffs the piece of card with my name back into his tartan holdall. And then he is bending down to hug me, this great big bear of a man, who, with his wife, Michelle, will take utmost care of me and lead me not astray –

I walk fast to keep in step with him and we load the luggage into the car and head for the supermarket to buy supplies.
Here, hold this – Biltong.
It's delicious.
Yep –

And then we're out of this asphalt jungle and Graham's driving too fast for my liking and on the sidewalk babies peer out of blankets tied to their mother's back and I squint my eyes up into a piercing sun, far into the horizon and there they are, splodges of turquoise, buried into the folds of every hill that we see.
African villages.
Yep.
See those three hogs of a mountain over there?
Yes.
Hogsback – Eastern Cape. You'll love it.

21 SEPTEMBER

The valley is named Tyume. It points eastwards deep into the bowers of the Eastern Cape. The River Kei is its master. Green sloping hills pour down onto its muddy banks, transformed into lowlands dotted with the huts of Xhosa folk.

I arch my neck backwards and stare up at the Hogs; its leader, Gaika's Kop, shoots up high into a sky where there is only one cloud. It has no competitor, dominating a ridge of toppling waterfalls and African pine.

And so I arrive at Nibelheim, on the outskirts of the village, to a wooden house on stilts, to a garden of azaleas, blossom, goldfinches and parrots, to a fairy tale world of dancing fat robins, where waterfalls steam like smoke in the air, birds, millions of them, flutter from branch to branch and delightful, delectable black shiny faces giggle at my skirts, grasping hold of my hands and pointing to the whiteness of my skin, running their fingers along it, in disbelief.

The garden is filled with conifers and Japanese cedar, magnolia and crab apples, spruce and flowering cherries. Rhododendrons bounce into my vision and tiny tangerine bell flowers, like the fuchsia in my garden pots back home, cascade down the edge of a stony path.

22 SEPTEMBER

I stop still in my tracks. Three tall silver birches, creviced with tissued bark, black as night, shaped like a diamond, block out my view. Branches stick out from the sides like chopped off leg stumps – like the old man from Bulungula, all skin and bone, whom I met two weeks later, tightening his fists on the arms of his wheelchair. Lost two legs in the Elandserand mine, 2007.

Nasty.

23 SEPTEMBER
BUT THIS IS HOGSBACK LAND

Cobalt blue turns into grey.

The silence is broken by the sound of a single bird chirping in the woodland. It is broken by a tap dripping into my sink. I throw open the curtains and then I see it – it was there, a whole world magnified and transformed by light. It burst its rays into my morning. I believed it would last. It is as if the ghost of Hogsback[47] has emptied her billycan of white thick boiling liquid and poured it over every tree and shrub and leaf and flower. I can see no more. Even the crow has gone to sleep. Ashes smoulder in the grate. The box of firelighters has disappeared. The twig basket is empty. There are no more logs. I bundle myself up in three jumpers and a poncho. I go back to bed. I cannot see a blessed thing. The mist creeps down, lower and lower.

24 SEPTEMBER

I am scrunched up in front of the fire, fingers freezing, warming my back and my feet and my shoulders, laying the wire netted tray on the floor and stuffing it up with more twigs and logs and Graham tells me not to worry –
There's loads of wood –
But it's wet!

I lift up the vase of scarlet buddleias, pink azaleas and polished olive leaves standing in the centre of my writing table, and move it to one side. I unzip one of the innumerable mesh cases stuffed full of technical computer devices and take out my memory stick.

It's only five o'clock in the afternoon. I have at least five hours ahead of me, undisturbed.

Endless.

25 SEPTEMBER

The blessed buzzing of the electricity wires is driving me barmy and I can't see further than one inch outside my bedroom window. A malachite chirps magnanimously midst a ring of dark green foliage, pushing its scent into the forefront of a circle of trees, foreboding, dark, mysterious. Graham saw three baboons yesterday, hiding in the shadows. I saw nothing.

But I'm a prisoner of my making here; not a soul knocks on the door. Old ladies turn to their bed at seven o'clock. Lovers shake themselves and flop back to sleep. This is Hogsback, swirling mists, black faces with toothless grins, old, paunched men, bent and shapeless, aproned women shuffling in slippers, baccis tearing up and down – backpackers exhausted, shivering, lying on their backs on an edge of a mountain.

The patterns continue. I rise at six, cold, struggling to lift my legs from the blankets and drawing open curtains to a still portrait of semi-darkness, fog and shadow, bush, stubble, tree and flower, wild seringa and African acorns, a living ring of abundance, creeping up into vision and then disappearing into nothing. This is the land of the hobbit –

I stumble over to the shower and turn on the hot tap, charging my system up as if I was pumping a million molecules of static electricity into my body.

I rub my bottom with a damp towel, dress in smelly, grubby clothes and trudge up to the end of the garden to give a plastic bag of dirty laundry to my hosts. Their wooded colonial home is a haven of civilisation, warm and cosy, with dogs sprawled out in every corner, munching biscuits and licking sores. Pippin, half-wolf, is king of this domestic menagerie.

I bury my face inside his hair.

26 SEPTEMBER

I have now seen my first yellowwood, Chinese maple, and knobwood. At seven a.m. I spot a blue crane with bulbous head and long wing-plumes. At eleven, a Cape robin prances onto my front lawn and plunges his beak into a mass of yellow dandelions. And this afternoon, Michelle takes her hand off the steering wheel and nudges me in the ribs. A kynsna lourie, crested head and salacious scarlet red bill, hops onto a fallen branch. Sunbirds zoom across the sky, amethyst and gold –

Crested flycatchers, red-necked spurfowls, knysna turaco and dark-backed weavers.

Birds are my princes now. I spy on them through binocular lenses, camouflaged as a professional bird-spotter. In secret I am merely an amateur voyeur, prying on their vulnerability. Their beauty does not age.
Until I shoot –
And they drop.
My dream.
No one else's.

I will follow the route of my ancestors, in my own way –
Alone.
Staring at crisp blue skies.
Musing on the stories.
Lying back on a cushioned chair.
Hearing the hum of the deafening cicadas.

27 SEPTEMBER

The sun hangs low, deceptively warm, seducing me to bundle up all my papers and sit at the small circular blue table on the veranda, to sip rooibos tea and melt into the timelessness of an African afternoon. But a sharp wind elbows its way into the small of my neck, into the grey ashes of damp wood and old wood shavings, into a hearth that needs little children, shiny black, to sit cross-legged and tell their stories, of frogs and hobbits, mushrooms and toads.

And then I see it – Mr Carpenter is his name; a voluptuous orange bumblebee with black strip on belly, zooming backwards and forwards across the helter-skelter of a pink and white blossomed sky.

28 SEPTEMBER

Shosh, I'll meet you at the gate tomorrow at six a.m. – Okay, I'll be there.

The sky, tinged with mauve, is still floating under a net of mist. A cock crows from afar over the hills and the sharp-cut edges of overgrown grass dampen the canvas sides of crumpled walking boots.

And in the cracks of space between three oak trees, a huge mountain, rising precipitously up into the sky, black, brooding and anonymous. I trudge on, trying to keep up with Graham. But it is a lost battle until he stops. It is always sudden, always when you least expect it. He places his finger over his mouth and utters not a word, merely lifting his binoculars to his eyes and craning his neck up high, high into the foliage of an *opregte geelhout*, the yellowest tree in town – eight hundred whopping years old.

A weaver flaps its wings and then it is gone, lost into the dense magic of a witch's forest. A sunbeam shoots across the trailing branches of a eucalyptus tree and I am twisting my head, arching my back, caressing the bark of a California redwood, transfixed by this brave new world where one only plays homage to the kingdom of birds –
Except when one is interrupted!
Maurice.
Why are you ringing now?
Six thousand miles away –
For God's sake.

Back in my room in Nidelheim, I unfasten the zip of a faded green canvas walking bag and pull out a piece of old man's beard. I push my hand down into one of the pockets and pull out a porcupine quill. It is sharper than a sewing needle. I sigh and gasp with pleasure at the smooth coverlet on my bed. Ndleka dusted the whole house this morning and swept the hearth.

★

Graham walks over to the washing line, carrying a plastic bowl filled to the brim with sopping wet socks, jumpers and T-shirts. Michelle watches him with a sharp eye.

South African women stand for no nonsense.
We train them well.
Any messin', then it's a leg in their arse and out the back door.

★

Ndleka's mother, Mafika, hums quietly to herself, checks to see how many candles she has made, opens a door and walks over to the cow barn to heat the wax. When it is warm and glowing, she returns to her seat, sits back, rests her spectacles on her nose and turns to the Bible.

29 SEPTEMBER

The sun sparkles –

Hogsback is teeming with visitors. They hover around the lawns in front of the teahouse on the village green, craning their necks up high to get the best view –

A dancer pirouettes across a courtyard – once, twice, three times and more! Her garments are flimsy, barely covering skin that glistens and gleams in its black nakedness. More appear, arching their backs like caterpillars and splitting their legs open wide, bending hips into distorted shapes and twirling into dancing cheetahs.

Veterans of the village spit into their handkerchiefs, toss their apple cores into a clump of lavender and move on.

I tuck Michelle's jumper into my trousers again for the seventy-ninth time, rush over to a village stall and buy smoked salmon and trout pâté, tangy sauces and apricots preserved in rich orange syrup and African milk cake. I stuff vegetable quiche and red wine into my rucksack, slide my hands across pottery with rich brown glazes, slip my arm around Michelle's waist and pull off her hat, tossing it into a bush of crimson roses.

We slump down, exhausted, onto a patch of mossy grass and sleep.

30 SEPTEMBER

Anton!
I can't see the road.
Oh my God – look!
An owl, hanging from the branch, swinging –

Graham's friend, Anton, steers the car slowly back up the lane, shining his headlights onto the two gates that I need to padlock together. I turn to him and heave a sigh of relief. *Thank you!*

I race up the path to Nibelheim, my fingers shaking as I jam the key in the lock and wrench open the patio doors. What if there was a lion behind me –

I'm still bundled up in layers of jumpers, fleece, anorak and poncho, woollen hat, scarf and mitts. Saturday night fever has bestowed its magic on me. I grab the mobile and text Laurel –

This was Broadway darling, in Africa, Starways Bar, wattle and daub, where the moon spearheads light onto a black and white film set, Ginger Rogers and Fred Astaire. Punters sprawl out under tall, spindly pine trees stretching up into sky that's studded with diamonds, and young girls strut around like peacocks, lifting their skirts, warming their toes, trampling the ash, steaming, into wet, pulsating slime.

And you know what, Graham speaks Zulu and Afrikaans.

★

A black-headed oriole screeches and flutters off into
the branches of a eucalyptus tree.
I press the 'on' switch of the electric blanket to high.
I want to go home.

1 OCTOBER

I still need to understand.
The story.
Thousands of Jews, embarking on a passage to Africa.
Lithuanian immigrants.
Desperate.

Teeming rain spills into the undergrowth.
Two hours later, the earth is steamy, scorching hot.
I am done in –
The village school lies ahead of me.
Young boys gather mushrooms in the woods.
I grit my teeth and plod on –

THE HEADMASTER INVITES ME FOR TEA

The Story of the Seaman unfolds.

'Teach a black man to be a plumber and when his boss dies, instead of carrying on the business, he goes back to being a gardener. The Kaffirs were uneducated, like Zuma – the man never went to school, hypnotised followers in the same way that Hitler did.'

'You were headmaster of a mission school?'

'Yes. The teachers are uncommitted. They come to Hogsback to be gardeners. If you don't give them work, they walk back to their families with heads down, humiliated. A man with no job is a nothing. As for the Jews, you know their story. Hundreds of them, clambering down the ramps from the ships, running around with dazed faces until some wagoner picked them up. Slept underneath, didn't care, shot hare or buck for a meal and walked non-stop until they reached the desert and diamond mines. Never stopped scrambling and searching, always searching for diamonds in huge crates embedded in a hill.'

His wife picks up the sun oven, a small metal bath with a mesh cover and strolls outside, placing it gently onto the stone floor of the verandah. Inside it she places an enamel bowl, filled with rice and water. She covers it with a black cloth. In a couple of hours, from the heat of the sun, the rice will be cooked.

'The sun is to be used,' she says.

The English lady is sweltering –

Shosh cuts herself a slice of potato bread and squeezes the juice of an orange into a plastic cup. She screws up her nose at the smell of rooibos tea, dreadful stuff. It's like drinking wet straw. A dog barks in the distance. A black gardener wheels a wheelbarrow over to the edge of the forest and digs for earth. A car swerves into the driveway of The Happy Hotel and a hand stretches out of the window to wave. A slow breeze stirs the trees.

2 OCTOBER

This is me, finding my way home.
To freedom.
Knowing what I need.
Not just what I want.

I haul myself out of a bed, submerged by blankets and duvets to a light that is immense. It changes, like a dream – the sun and the blue and the shades of grey, the wisteria, lavender, cascading down onto a Juliet balcony, the sense of Baloo, my horse, underneath me, gentle, knowing of my trepidation and placing his feet, one in front of the other, carefully, slowly onto the path in front of us, the pines of this huge magnificent forest looming up like a hundred Christmas trees glued together – dogs chasing and playing, dappled light midst the trees – this was a madness, my thighs learning to tighten muscle and grip on his bare sensuous back, my hands clutching the leather of a tiny, tiny saddle, learning to be free with the reins, adjusting, trusting that Baloo would look after me and not let me fall – but ooh, my bum was getting sore and wheeeeeeeeeee – we were going downnnnnnnnnnn, down, down and I gripped him so hard.

'Place your feet up a little from the stirrup!' he shouted – 'lean backwards' and then Baloo was munching grass and not paying attention and suddenly, suddenly, without any warning he was trotting and my bum was being lifted up to the sky and I called out to the horseman and told him that this was my meditation, a meditation to the upper heavens of life.

3 OCTOBER

Shosh, you can't walk on your own.
Why not?
Baboons.

4 OCTOBER

The sky is coated with thick, thick black paint. I shine the torch on a gravelled path. Not a living creature, leaf or flower stirs. The Garden of Eden is sleeping.

I wake to a shroud of mist and see nothing apart from luminous shadow silhouettes of blossom, oak and vine. *Lord of the Rings* is master here. I smile, remembering the guys last night, laughing and joking. Graham stoked the *Braii.*

Wood and charcoal sizzled, pushed up against blackened breasts of chicken, butternut squash wrapped in silver foil and vegetarian sausages; on the tables, Pyrex dishes filled voluptuously with potato bake, coleslaw, succulent salad and glasses of sweet ginger wine that soaked a thirst of a hundred years, notwithstanding waffles with maple sauce and ice cream, conversation that spurted back and forth and a vision of Cape Town cut into sections and pencilled out on paper.

All life descends from the mountain.

5 OCTOBER

I climb into the bacci with Graham. Feel like a tramp. Need to wash my hair – flops onto my face like wet spaghetti. We stop to ask a black man where he's going with a bin liner of rubbish slung over his shoulder. 'I'm going home' he says.

What's going on, Graham?
They have a habit of stealing rubbish
and then filling the bag up with their own crap.
Can't afford rubbish bags.
Live from hand to mouth.

I shudder.
Feel uncomfortable.
He's discriminating.
I don't like the smell.

6 OCTOBER

I grab hold of Michelle and kiss her on her lips.
Shosh –
Yes.
I pull her body towards me.
She grips hold of her stick –
Rheumatoid arthritis eats into her bones.

You will come back.
Yes.

I pack my rucksack, sling it over my shoulder and stick my thumb out to hail down a lift. A bacci skids to a halt, crunching its fallen exhaust pipe over the potholes as if it had the hiccups and shooting out stones, left, right and centre. I scoot round to sit next to the driver. Time to move on.
Not good in Cape Town.
Bad.
Everyone lives behind bars.

I go to Bulangula
first.

Don't forget to peel three cloves of garlic twice a day and stick 'em in a glass of milk. Keeps the ticks away.
Yes sir!
Clicks his big white teeth and tells me to be careful.

GUANI GAMA LAKHO?
What is your name?

I sit in the back of a pick-up truck. My knees are hunched up and squashed against the legs of the man opposite me. His name is Benjamin. He has a gentle face. He is thin like a rake. Tells me he is recovering from tuberculosis. He goes home to visit his mother. We surge forward, driving through dipping hills and valleys, and I stare through a dirty window at the random washes of purple and red, streaking a sky that has been left out in the rain. The grey leaves of eucalyptus trees brush against the wooden sides of a trailer, filled to the brim with sacks of potatoes and rice, paraffin oil, plastic bowls, mattresses, broken chairs and cardboard boxes of chillies and carrots, cabbage and pepper.

We pass through small towns that lead to nowhere. Africans squat and gossip. I see a man, bent forward, clutching a walking stick. A stray dog tears open a bag of maize. The rain lashes down. Women with bare feet cover themselves up in black dustbin liners. Nothing will be left to chance. Even the trash of the local municipality is laid out for pickings.

Olitto, the owner of the truck, yanks the gearstick into neutral and swerves. Benjamin throws his arms out to stop me from falling. The truck spins round ninety degrees. A clod of earth splatters onto the back seat window. A lizard slides onto the spoke of a wheel and falls asleep. A young woman, wrapped in a thick blanket, throws a bunch of spinach root onto the driver's face. I stretch out my hand to touch her cheek. It is covered in clay – white. I push a sack of sugar beet to one side and force open the door. The road is a mess, full of potholes and stinking shit, poured without purpose onto scrubland that plummets down into sand dune and forest. It is pitch black.

Three men dig us out.

7 OCTOBER

The land is breathtaking. It is remote. It is Bulungula – open grass stretches to a skyline, soft to the touch, falling in grace over the speckled hills and dales of African homesteads – it lies within the village of Nqileni on the Wild Coast. There is no piped water. Drinking water is drawn from unprotected springs in the ground. I am in hut five, a circular wattle and daub hut, a rondawel. It is bright turquoise. I love it.

I hang my jeans over a wooden bar, nailed to the inside wall. I hear a chicken squawking. A woman in a long, cotton aproned dress, knocks on my door and says

Kujani.

Eight a.m., I pick up a small container of paraffin, pour it into a teapot, try not to spill it, and pour the liquid into a hole at the bottom of a tall metal pipe. I cover it with two sheets of toilet paper and light it with a burner. The water is hot now. I undo my bra and pull down my pants. I hook them onto a nail in the wall.

Uhmm – these Xhosa women are tough old girls. They grind twenty cobs of fresh maize every day and boil it up into *puto*. I couldn't do it.

But the rhythm of life is good for me –

White waves of surf roll over each other, each one moving the ocean, inch by inch, back, back towards Antarctica. I scoop up clams and octopus. Birds swoop down over the water reflecting a misty shadow of the village above. Dense foliage greets me on the path to my hut and the patter of continuous rain dampens my back and wets my shoes. Backpackers sit in silence in a communal hut. They read or surf the net.

Some write home to lovers. A black woman strokes the shape of my legs – *full.*

I gather firewood with Nijinala and rinse spinach and cabbage, washing the leaves in two bowls of water. She fingers my hair and tries to braid it. She looks like my grandmother. She sits on a patch of grass beside the fire, legs outstretched, stirring a pot of beans and smoking a hookah. She gazes at my left hand.

Nijinala, how many cows am I worth? I ask her and then she's grabbing hold of my arm and dragging me across dried-up patches of grass and pushing open the door of the wattle and daub church painted in apricot and introducing me to Big Mama and they're all over me, crowds of them, dressed in traditional isiXhosa costumes, eyes rolling, mouths open, swaying and clapping, welcoming me, tying a skirt onto my hips, parading the cross up and down.

If I lost track of God, this is where I'd find him.

MAMA TOFU[48]
Ngxingxolo

Tell me about love, Mama Tofu.

She clicks her tongue.
The Xhosa way.
I wait.

It is a mystery, this love, but first you must ask the man questions and if he gives you good answers, he is a good man and he will be good to you. And above all, ask him about sex. What is it for? Is the pleasure merely for him or merely for her? Do they join, together?

She rolls her eyes up towards the heavens, draws them to a close, places her hands on her hips, and sways gently from side to side.

Our boys have circumcision rituals which makes them men. At fourteen they are cut.

I nod my head.
We cut at birth.

We sacrifice ox when man dies. And when man and woman marry, the man must pay labola. Eight cows – richness is measured through cows and daughters.

It is wise to have structure, I say.

A small child sits cross-legged in the corner, scratching himself.
The men sit on tree stumps in the *kraal* talking.
The women do not join them.
I have much to learn –

I begin to doze in the warmth of the sun. Rivulets of sweat run down my face. A fly buzzes in my ear. I step into the shade of my rondawel and collapse on the bed.

8 OCTOBER

In the fading light of an early evening, I clutch hold of Nozanatini and Nijinala, wipe away the moistness in their eyes and climb into the taxi, front seat. They stay. I go.
Cintsa?
Yes please –
Tonight.

★

Unspoilt white sand, backed by forested dunes, lagoons and rivers stretches out to a horizon of still water, unmoving. I stand transfixed – and fall, spreading my legs like strips of seaweed into the water below.

9 OCTOBER

I tell you Laurel.
It's awesome here, awesome.

If I don't see water piddling into my little wooden cabin in about half an hour, then the Lord God is showin' real mercy on us down here in Africa. It's just plotzin' down – we're all slippin' and slitherin' around like tadpoles. Pretty pointless wearin' shoes and as for clothes, forget it – we might just as well walk round in our birthday suits. I wouldn't be surprised if that Indian Ocean down there won't be taking me surfin' in the morning and I best be careful 'cause I've got to take a plane at twelve o'clock over to the Western Cape and you know something, they all said –
Come in the spring, best time –
All the flowers are bloomin', country is as pretty as a picture. Well, I don't know any more. I've lost my faith in what people say. I'm just goin' to read my Bible and listen to the Lord.

10 OCTOBER

I have lost sense of time. Rain is bucketing down, pounding on the corrugated roof of a shack that is wooden and African women talk of babies and dig their fingers into shopping bags zigzagged with stripes and curl their feet over damp couches from flaking ceilings and white froth stretches out into a sea that goes on for ever. Young girls bend down to dry the skin between their toes, prancing back to a wooden counter, grabbing knives to cut up carrots and onions, grating beetroot and skinning fish, boiling the *kishkes*[49] of chicken and steaming rice –

Feeding families.
Always a family.
I watch them – solid
not in between.

But I do have a family.
My own one.
I don't have to feel like that.
Solitary.
I tear off a sheet of paper and write.
We need to communicate.
Not be silent.
Understand our past and present.
Give the narrative time to heal.

BODHI KHAYA

The name combines the ancient language of Sanskrit with isiXhosa. It is a place for awakening one's spirit to possibility –

The taxi-driver skids to a halt on a rutted gravel track, pulls on the gearstick hard. I haul my luggage out from the boot, clutching bags of supplies, a loaf of rye and a jar of sundried peaches. I step over a patch of earth, filled with daffodil and lily and swing round to see a mountain, tall and foreboding, swathed in mist, rising above an old Dutch settlement cottage, buried into a landscape that nestles at the foot of the Witkransberg. It is called the *Ha-de-da*.

Whitewashed and perfect, open fireplace, stacked with logs, piles and piles of logs. A roof strung with reeds, bamboo blinds, comfy chairs, Afghan rugs, wooden chests, bookcases, saucepans, pans, forks, spoons, everything one could possibly need. Tonight I pick salad leaves, chard and fresh herbs for my supper and steam rice with tomato sauce. Rhythm of life is still. I write little. I cannot force it. It will be strange to return to England. I have not seen a soul for two days.

Perdita knocks on the door to bring me two stamps. Embers smoulder in a log fire. My walking shoes are placed in front of it to dry. They are sodden. Late this afternoon, as the sun lowers over the valley, I sip tea and stare through the window at lime green weavers, turning upside down like babies and fluttering in the trees. The homestead is a sanctuary.

Baboons are barking. They plunge down the mountain side. No signal on my mobile phone. A bushbuck stops me in my tracks.

I jump from boulder to boulder, free as a fairy, picking at wild asparagus with spreading spines, treading on gorse and leaf, spiked and sharp, scooping up yellow dandelions and pale blue flowers, bowing my head before the King Protea, single-stemmed and erect –

★

Heat waves bounce off the road ahead and I ride through pincushions, silver-edged, up to the middle of wide open mountains, my bum stuck to a saddle that is merely a slab of leather, thrown onto the horse's back –

★

Zadeka waddles off across the lawn, carrying mops and buckets. An English man named Tom pushes a wheelbarrow full of stones. An ageless woman, with curly hair, rests her straw hat on top of the piano and plays Beethoven's Fifth...

Perhaps I will stay –

THE MAN WITH THE HOMBURG HAT

Philip Bendel, 1932

CAPE TOWN

'Could have bought it for a hundred pounds'
He used to say –

Philip Bendel, Esquire, the man who sailed to London with a black coat and a Homburg hat, the millionaire who flew the flag for socialism but paid out lousy wages, the plutocrat who became the first Jewish mayor of Finsbury, the step-grandfather who burnt my sister's hand with a fat cigar, the lover, who on the last day of mourning for his missus, proposed marriage to my grandmother, is this morning, at precisely seven twenty-five a.m., drenching me in sweat, because I want to know...

i.e. – Patricia Har-Even
Carol Susan Nathanson

What it was it like.
When he sailed for the first time.
To Cape Town.
To South Africa?

I have no letters.
His childhood in Rokiskis.
His youth.
His entanglements
expunged into history.

I will write them for him.
A selection.
Hand-picked.

I will chart his story.
What is it that pulls me?
The echo of repetition in the characters.
Natasha and Philip.
Maurice and Shosh.

THE SEAMAN
The beginning of a Jewish story
One of many
1880–1910

To my darling Goddess, Natasha… my childhood sweetheart,

A crescent of a moon appeared in my window tonight and I will pack my bag, with caution and ease, following the line of its movement. I have now completed all necessary preparations for the journey and I will say goodbye, with not a shadow of doubt about the wisdom of my decision to leave Rokiskis… I have the support of all my family.

Sleep on board with me, Natasha. I know it's a dream. But it's the best way, for the sea air is bracing and fills the body with all that has been lost. The light of day is patched with a jigsaw of colour and I am mesmerised by the plume of a wave, rising, soaring at least forty feet into the air. I open my mouth wide. I wish you were here, I really do.

But I knew this was right. I had no choice. When we anchored at the edge of the sea shore, on the bank of the largest ocean in the world, and I passed a boy walking, knowing no other life than the rhythm of its turning, watching the sails coming in and going out. I knew that like him, I was the happiest man alive… a seaman, removed from the drabness of life in Lithuania.

★

The swish of the water, the rolling and pitching, the sweat pouring off me in rivulets is just indescribable and then I nearly lose my footing, whilst craning my neck up high to look at three shrunken masts. They remind me of the broomsticks in my poor mama's corner closet. I perch my body on a piece of rope and lean backwards, ravenous with hunger and then the harpooners and boat steerers are screaming at me to get back down on my knees to scrub the decks and, six hours later, the sky is darkening and casting shadows over my face but I daren't look up in case a steward gives me a kick in the arse and I can't tell you enough times, from the core of my heart that I'm bleating with terror like a sheep inside me and desperate to catch my breath and just take one moment, one minute, to look up at the moon. Then it disappears and all light is blotted out.

One night I could not sleep and stood looking out onto a sea that was calm and placid, where the brilliance of a moon glared its glory onto a silver trail of water that stretched right up to the horizon; but it does not last. Nothing does. It just changes, like our lives. It disappoints... For then the ship's bowsprit and jibboom suddenly tilts to one side and I'm scampering down the deck, sliding from side to side, slipping on the litters of cargo that are to be found in every nook and cranny, for now the sea is foaming and boiling like a cauldron and the men are disgruntled and exhausted, scooping up water in buckets and running out of energy and blindly clutching a ladder, I struggle to get back down and escape from this torrent of wind that will kill us all.

★

When the sea turns my stomach Natasha, I just want to die into oblivion. It is utter misery, I am a crazed animal.

My berth is no bigger than a rabbit hutch. Often I lie there, folded up like a snail beneath a rough blanket, before building up the courage to go back on deck again and stare transfixed at the multitude of fish that sometimes entwine themselves within the incursion of thick slimy seaweed that lays its entrails over waves that dip and dive in between and up and down, never-ending and infinite in their rhythms.[50]

I am not fed well – but my stomach is taut, strong, hard as nails. Starting to chew tobacco like everyone else, I pry into holes and corners. I crawl into the main hatch, under the longboat. A spindly sailor with a broken leg grabs hold of my ear and teaches me how to knot and splice. Gentle breezes caress my face. Sandflies get up my nose. I gaze, spellbound at this tropical sea which goes on forever and ever...

One of the skippers, Joe is his name, beckons me over to lie under a piece of canvas with him. His face is gaunt and the smell of tobacco from his mouth disgusting, but I listen to his stories and utter not a word.

The wind is steady and southerly. Another day and we should see the Cape.

★

The seaman squints his eyes up into the foggy white haze of Table Mountain.

'Is that it?' he whispers to Joe.

It is a perpendicular mountain. It is a mass of rock and stone, sliced off at the top – interwoven with butterfly trees, wild seringa and geranium. It threatens the living daylights out of every creature that comes near. He shudders, catching his breath, swallowing saliva, ready to dive overboard like an octopus and plant his feet on African soil.

He runs, daring not to look back, panting, watching the breath spiral out of his mouth like wisps of snow, diving down to hide under the shade of an evergreen, pulling off the torn shirt from his soaked back and tying it round his waist, shivering, pushing himself through the blistering bush of this foreign land...

He rubs the sleep from his eyes and watches the wagons, six of them, pulled by sixteen oxen and driven by one man. One lash of a whip and all hell is let loose. The cries of a whimpering child echo in his ears. A woman screams in terror. A man shouts. It is a language of his past. It is Yiddish.

The canvas flap of a wagon is pushed aside and a woman steps out, pulling her skirts up and taking care not to slip on the muddied earth. She is bundled up in a ragged green skirt with at least two or three woollen shawls slung carelessly across her shoulders. Her eyes are dark, dreamy, mirroring the wells from which my grandfather would draw water.[51]

The world inside her is hidden.

Her lips are full, moist with desire.

'Where are you from?' the seaman asks.

'Aoch... always they ask the Jews that question. From the Shtetlach, Rokiskis! Lithuania.' She leans back onto the side of the wagon and her eyelids droop. 'Uhmm, what would you know...'

⋆

I am merely a child. It is in the fifties...

I watch my mother from the corner of my eye. She sighs. Shakes her head from side to side, trembles. It is a gesture that requires no words, a purse of the lips, that sums up the whole experience of her Jewish identity. I recognise it in my grandmother, when she taps her fingers on the side of her nose. I was brought up with it. Questions were not to be answered.

⋆

Natasha,

I kept thinking of you all, when she spoke of our childhood, running out when the sun had barely risen to steal apples from peasant orchards, and you, crouched down on your bottom with your face buried in your hands, not daring to look... Watching Zalman, the way he kept his head down, bent over like a horse, swinging his fingers back and forth like the branches of a willow tree. I thought of all the people we grew up with... Itzik, the forest businessman, Leibe the barkeeper, Shmuel the sexton, Hirshl, the tailor, Zuse, the teacher of cheder[52] *and the sweet smell of baby milk, bubbling away in your mother's samovar that held at least thirteen cups of water.*

★

Natasha pores over Philip's letter, slowly, struggling to decipher the words. Her mother snatches it from her, holding it up to the light of a candle. Her daughter's cough is troublesome. She prays that all will be well. Natasha is losing heart. Time is against her now. She is losing the battle to join him.

★

The woman continues…

'The *landsleit*[53] told us to go to Cape Town, to look for our relatives. Everyone was screaming, shouting… My father running into the road, small children perched on the back of the wagon. Nobody could believe it, my mother shaking so much that even the soldiers couldn't still her.'

'We leave the *shtetl* on a Sunday… Seven days it takes us to get to Liepaja! And then we board the ships… Cargo boats! Aaach, my stomach. We were treated like *vilde khayes* – wild animals, pigs, sleeping on dung, and then with the boat rolling and pitching like nobody's business, the captain hauls a barrel of salt herrings onto the deck, throws down a dirty sack of boiled potatoes, and kicks over a bucket stuffed to the brim with dried up chunks of black bread.'

'Fress!'[54,55]

'And then after many days, after arriving in London, the docks, the Jewish poorhouse, the waiting and waiting, we clamber on to a steamship to South Africa. Nineteen days of weather. I pencilled them off on a piece of card. Blizzards slice the skin from your face and push you over to the railings. Decks are littered with bodies, bent into two, spewing out the remains of a meal, not worth mentioning. The stench is disgusting. It was enough, I tell you. Enough.

'Three weeks we live like this. And then we saw it. I clutched hold of the railings. It rose from the sea. I was terrified. We did not know of such a thing, covered in white. We grabbed hold of each other. Even my husband was still...

'This was our Statue of Liberty.'

'This... but then the captain is screaming at us, his voice thunderous, bellowing out like a foghorn, yelling at us to rush down the gangplank and ten big, strapping men, round us up like cattle and lead us to the bathhouse, slosh buckets of water over our heads to get rid of the lice, cut the hair from our faces, give us cloth for our bodies. *'Griner'*, they call us... *'Griner'*.[56]

'We trudge behind the boss in a queue, two by two like the animals in Noah's ark and they give us a room to rent which has no air or light and the walls are black, grimy, smelling, stinking and the cracks are stuffed up with pebble and stone, stalk and nettle. Windows are broken, filled with crackling newspaper and the doors filled with so many holes, that if Hymie, my husband, comes near to me again in such a godforsaken place, I'll shove him back into his trousers and find me a Boer man to rest my head on. They read the same Bible as us.

'And I tell you something else, the men never have time to eat. Always on the run, to save money... searching for some old *shmutters*[57], sacks, bottles, lumps of meat... ribs, tongue, nothing too fatty... anything, so that they can become a 'tryer'... just to save money. *'Kishke gelt'*[58,59] I used to say to Hymie.

'But we look after each other. I still run my hands down his aching back into the crevices and rub his feet and clutch hold of his chest in the middle of night... And the wind soars high, high into a crescendo, howling and hammering on my door, and the shadow of a lizard spins across the window pane.'

The seaman can listen no more.
He wanders off into the sunset.
The nights are cold.
He cannot survive on wits alone.
He must eat.

Dearest Natasha,
I do not know if this letter will ever reach you but my loneli-

ness is slowly killing me. It is now two years…

In the early hours of dawn, before the sun spills sunlight onto my naked shoulders, I place a heavy pack upon my back, just like a pedlar, bound with leather and string and ride out into the karoo. My name is Smous[60] *now. I am no longer skin and bone – the boy from the sea is fattening up! I have sold my donkey back to the Boer and now own a horse and a wagon. I sell meat and bread, tablecloths and napkins, blankets, herrings, knives, forks, graters – anything you could possibly imagine, sweetheart. Even ostrich feathers and ostrich eggs! But the flies drive me crazy and as for the blacks –*

I'm learning to manage them.

★

Yesterday I harnessed Jeremiah onto a wooden strut and stroked the flank of his ample backside. I tied the ropes of my wagon around the buttocks of a sawn off tree trunk and hobbled out across the market. I needed a drink – fast. The South African sun is relentless. I wiped the sweat from my brow, kicking aside a jagged rock and spitting onto the red glinting stone. I pushed aside a drunkard, bumped into a couple of makeshift hustlers and walked tentatively over to an open, bare piece of land, crammed full of losers from every corner of this earth. Rows of tents spill out onto a distant horizon. There's no charity here, but fall into a diamond mine at Kimberley and you'll never come out. As for the Kaffirs, most of them end their lives down there, pushin' and pullin' trolleys of earth.[61] *Have to say, Natasha, I was tempted to go down… Filch a diamond or two, slip it between my fingers and hide it in my back pocket… Just imagine, my beautiful one… If I bought shares in the diamond mine for a low price and sold them for a high one.*

★

But you know something Natasha, the Boers are better at this game than we are. We're learning how to survive in this wild country, but they know, deep inside their guts, how to do it. They seem closer to God than our lot. It's different. They resemble the Hebrew patriarchs.

And they are good men and help me. Yesterday, I have to say, that I lost hope and at the crack of dawn, whilst boiling up tea in a metal canister, a Boer crouched down beside me, crossed his legs and pressed his hand in my hand. I bit my nails down to the quick and then told him about you, Natasha… about all the family, left in Lithuania. I told him how poor and destitute we were. He pulled me to him, wiping away a tear from underneath his eyes and offering me a bed for the night.

'My Joodje.'

He knew where I came from.

★

I will not forget you, Natasha. I will save money and return home. I will.

Please believe me. But I must tell you. I am abundant with energy today. The local farmer, a Boer, allows me to live on his open fields and cultivate his land. I can disappear for weeks and months, laden with sacks of merchandise in the wagon but know that I have a home to return to, when I am ready. Despite the relentless sun, it's a little paradise here. God shows us his mercy. Only yesterday, the skies opened and the rain fell, bucketsful. My vegetables are sodden and as to my fruits, I cannot describe to you the joy, when gathering up baskets over-flowing with apples, plums, peaches and wild blackberries, all to be munched and composted, jammed and juiced. The branches in the lower orchard are breaking off from the weight of the apples and I counted at least four varieties.

The only soreness, and it really irks me, is the fact that a liquor store opened up here, just a few months ago, and folk from villages, scattered for miles around, are barging in late at night, slamming doors and frightening the farmer's children. I have to say, aggression and disorderliness confounds me. I just don't understand it.

As for bringing in supplies, apart from a single dirt track, there's only one tarred road which runs right through the centre of the village. The potholes are horrendous. Many a time I've been catapulted into some stinking puddle or estuary bank clogged up with mud and nettles and then I'm covered from head to toe with a cloud of dust and the sound of hooves galloping away ringing in my ears and I'm splashing my arms and wetting my lips with a flask of water.

You'd love it here, Natasha, really love it. I am bewitched by waterfalls, greens and ancient forests.

But how can I bring you here?

'VANT TO PUY A VAATCH'[62]

Natasha –
I have had enough of 'peutiful tiamond prooches'
and being called a
'Boereverneaker'.
Enough.

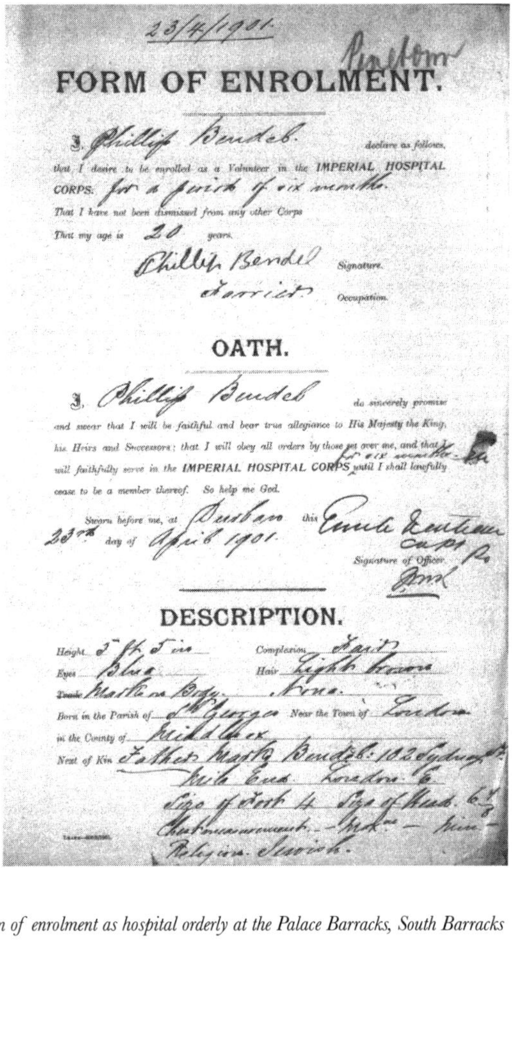

23/4/1901

FORM OF ENROLMENT.

I, Phillip Bendel declare as follows,
that I desire to be enrolled as a Volunteer in the IMPERIAL HOSPITAL CORPS. for a period of six months.
That I have not been dismissed from any other Corps
That my age is 20 years.

Phillip Bendel Signature.
Farrier Occupation.

OATH.

I, Phillip Bendel do sincerely promise and swear that I will be faithful and bear true allegiance to His Majesty the King, his Heirs and Successors; that I will obey all orders by those set over me, and that I will faithfully serve in the IMPERIAL HOSPITAL CORPS for six months until I shall lawfully cease to be a member thereof. So help me God.

Sworn before me, at Durban this 23rd day of April 1901.

Signature of Officer.

DESCRIPTION.

Height 5 ft 5 ins Complexion Fair
Eyes Blue Hair Light brown
Marks on Body. None.
Born in the Parish of St Georges Near the Town of London
in the County of Middlesex
Next of Kin Father Marks Bendel. 102 Sydney St. Mile End. London E.
Size of Boot 4 Size of Head 6⅞
Chest measurement
Religion Jewish.

Form of enrolment as hospital orderly at the Palace Barracks, South Barracks

The seaman sold his wagon, richly loaded with wine, butter, goat skins, feathers and oranges, puffed his chest up, scrubbed the grime from his knees, sluiced back his hair and on the 23rd April, 1901, enrolled as a hospital orderly at the Palace Barracks in Simonstown Bay, just east of Cape Town. A mere lad of twenty years.

He'd also accumulated, God knows how, numerous agricultural implements, a few sticks of furniture and a dozen or so bottles of patent medicines. One could never be sure –

All of this stuffed at the back of the wagon, under a huge hairy blanket. Gunpowder in vinegar was his favourite.

When they handed him a medal for his services at the end of the War, his mouth gaped open and he hung his head in shame. He was often sick himself – like many others, he had needed this period of life to convalesce from a deep hole inside him, an emptiness – and to halt the shaking of his body when he smelt the stench of surviving captured Boers and the shiver down his spine, the physical fear, unthinkable, that he too would be plagued with enteric fever. He had tried his utmost to earn respect from patients and nurses. But everyone knew, the women were better at this game. It was in their blood. Hearing the groans and racking coughs of men in mortal agony, observing the wards on the second and third floors, filled up with rows of narrow iron beds and delirious victims from the battle of Paardeberg[63], he just wanted to run.

★

To my darling goddess…

I admit my weakness. My stomach heaves when I see young boys bent in half, gouged by bayonets, Boers with dripping blood and bones that protrude from limbs, pulverised into mutilated pulp. And then for a split second of a moment, I stare with frozen eyes into nothingness, as strong and bold as the trees that swoop down over my window, beyond and below the great wall of Table Mountain. I know not how to feel. It is a reality that is senseless but so is death.

And then to comfort myself Natasha, in the middle of the middle of our two separate lives, with a whole world of space in between, with vulnerability, laughter and not even a pinprick of embarrassment, I ask you merely to let my hand follow the length of your back, and to say hello, to touch you everywhere, between your legs and between your buttocks and let me cry, so that when I push into you, into the deep crevice of my cowardice, I can shake like a man who has had his throat cut, because soon I must leave South Africa.

I have to.

But first, let us be together here, leave Rokiskis, and bury your head inside the crux of my arm as we doze together under the shade of a mimosa tree. You see, September will still be sunny and warm and the leaves, rampant.

Yet I forget. It just happens. My life takes over. You live in another land, across the sea, the sun draws to a fateful close.

I have not bathed since Tuesday, and my forehead,

let alone my knees, is a maze of cuts and grazes. I must warn you though, we will need mosquito nets over our beds in the summer but please do not fret. The ways of this country will soon be as familiar to you as a Lithuanian stebl, *but I have to say, you would have scratched your head in disbelief if you had seen us (a whole group of ward orderlies) crouched round the camp fire, swatting flies, gorging on buck, and having a heated discussion on land settlements.*

Just to get away one night from the stench of over 800 sick and wounded men – what difference where they come from, Boers, Kaffirs –

The senselessness of war.

Sweet goddess –
Do you remember how to kiss?

★

I cannot describe to you the excitement of seeing Table Bay again. The endless hours, days, of trying to survive in the Karoo, being so alone, has exhausted me. Dried-up river beds and watercourses, no streams, no waterfalls, nothing.

But now, with a gale of heat grazing my face, a wind that straddles you with red dust and the sound of a wild sea smashing into broken rock along the quayside, I am glad to say that leaving Rokiskis and coming to South Africa was the right decision –

If not, in retrospect, a tortuous one.

Hundreds of ships, men-of-war, and transports occupy every inch of my horizon. It is breathtaking. Each troopship has a painted number on its side. The decks swarm with half-naked black boys. Every road, packed to the brim with the fatigued faces of khaki-clad infantry and cavalry.

We hear heart-rending stories, of men marching for five days, without supplies, of barely slipping off their horses to rest, of swilling water into parched throats and then collapsing.

★

Natasha,

I have to tell you, my dreams were so vivid this morning, I couldn't even open my eyes, but just as one of the sentries shoved his rifle in my back and told me to get going, I found myself thinking of the Dutch farmer I'd met in the karoo. He'd had twenty-one children… fourteen sons and seven daughters. He was a rich man and his greatest happiness was to visit his family, who were now spread out, living in different farms in the neighbourhood. His handsome wife, vigorous, bosoms falling from beneath her blouse, was now in her sixtieth year, and regretting that she hadn't had more children![64]

Lyb g'tyn,

Will that be our future –

But I mustn't digress from what is in front of me. The grounds of the Palace Barracks have been filled with tents to accommodate hospital offices and field kitchens. Prisoners of war lie on straw palliasses, either under canvas with a tarpaulin or in a hut with gauze screens to keep away the flies. The huts are stuffier and not as well ventilated as the tents.

The sun scorches us. If I brush my arm against the canvas, it feels like boiled rubber. The insects are horrendous. They crawl over your skin and pick on the pus of open wounds like babies on a woman's nipple.

It is disgusting.

If nothing else, the British Army will not go hungry. Their military supply tents are filled to the brim with bags of mealies and oats, bales of lucerne and oathay, boxes of biscuits, bully beef, jam and other rations.[65] *I have acquired a taste for rooibos tea – soothes the catarrh in my throat. It's quite cheap, grown in the Cedarberg. You can buy a grainbag full, weighing seventy-five pounds, for about twopence to fourpence a pound.*

I cannot sleep, Natasha. It is four a.m. in the morning. I try to snuggle down but there is a pain in my bladder. I dream of sliding into you. The inner tent is sagging. I must tighten the ropes and take care not to trip over a large stone or a tree stump.

Shell and rifle fire never stops. The British claim to be 1600 strong, on an almost open plateau, stretching far into the horizon, beyond the ridges of Table Mountain.

They were covered by artillery and rifle fire from three sides, with shells bursting at a rate of seven per minute. We hear stories of Boers coming right up to soldiers' faces and fighting hand to hand.

Perhaps I should go outside and check the guy ropes. The group of orderlies that I belong to will be on duty in an hour. I have to tell you my sweet, sweet lyb g'tyn, that I pull in my stomach, tensing the muscle that wants to pee. I don't want to pee. I want to sleep. I want to feel your arms tight around my neck.

You are older now.
Are there lines on your face?

★

Men are buried in their thousands –
Spade-diggers pierce their forks into brown clogged earth; the day is wet, mucky and depressing.

NATASHA
Turn of the century
Rokiskis

Philip,
You are right –
It is deepest winter here.

When will you come home?

There is a shaking in me, quite inexplicable, that rises up through my body to a patch of skin just below my neck, that makes me feel quite like sixteen again and I would not wish dear Philip, for you to take me for granted.

I do not pay attention to the change of time. But when blackness disappears, I am torn in half, wanting your body to turn to me. Yesterday, I imagined you were with me and I grabbed your arm, pulling you over to an overloaded wooden barrow of shmutters and trinkets. It was market day. Rokiskis was teeming; men in black garb, jostling and hustling, backwards and forwards and then I saw this tablecloth. I said to you, 'That is the one I want and no other' and you asked me if it was long and wide and was it embroidered with lace and did it remind me of Mama. She always placed a tablecloth on the table.

Philip,

It is Sunday evening. Six o'clock. The wind howls. I remember your voice. It is yours, is it not? How can I forget. I try to be generous, to understand. It is a yearning for your soul. It is a burden too heavy to bear.

You *left*.
You *ran away*.

And now I laugh, gurgling from inside the bit that is fighting to breathe, the bit that will not be strangled by your shadow. You *discarded me*.

I am contemptuous of your betrayal.

Natasha wrote many letters to Philip
pleading in vain for her lover's return.
A pointless exercise.
Illness is not an attractive attribute.
Life is short.
Pragmatism is always the winner.

*

In December 1907, my step-grandfather, Philip Bendel, aged twenty-seven, boarded a steamship belonging to the infamous Union-Castle Line. Identified both as a foreigner and boot maker, he was pushed below decks into steerage. The heat was abominable and sweat poured in rivulets down his underarms and over his chest. The stench of sewage made him throw up. An old man, soaked to the skin, clung on to a metal railing, spewing his guts out, sobbing.

A child with no mother sat alone in the bow of the ship, water swilling around her ankles like nobody's business. Was the ship going down?

She cried out, leaning her back against a pile of hessian sacks, surrounded by creaking timbers and stinking crates. Philip ignored her.

He'd been advised to only take on board such articles as knives, forks, spoon, bedclothes, sewing machine, candles, matches and other small things.

His own list, however, was more expansive. It included a coveted black overcoat and a Homburg hat.

After the war the Boers rebuilt South Africa. But the Jews still held the gold. They became citizens of the land. But the seaman, born and bred in Lithuania, gave up on his attempt to have a share of it. He had left his family in Rokiskis, abandoned Natasha, had a stab at being hardy, dabbled with beer-houses in Durban, taken a ship to Freemantle in Australia and finally travelled to London again to make his fortune as a smous, but this time a cleverer one.

In 1908, Philip Bendel traded as a boot dealer at 23 White Conduit Street, London. The business failed. He therefore disposed of his stock of boots and shoes to Aaron Marks of 6 White Conduit Street, from whom he received two bills, or promissory notes, payable at three months, for £88: one dated 4th October for £58 and the other dated 10th October, 1910, for £30.[66]

Then followed a history of dubious wheelings and dealings, shady business transactions, non-payment of creditors, false statements, misconstrued communications and a growing dread that maybe he'd got it wrong; should have stayed in Durban, haggling with the Kaffirs. Hard to imagine this stocky, rather fusty-smelling gentleman with fair complexion and light-brown hair hawking drapery from one side of the street to the other, being my step-grandfather. A man of many parts.

As I discovered, life was full of them.

When applying for British naturalisation, the Criminal Investigation Department of New Scotland Yard claimed that he was unable to produce any documentary proof of his travels in South Africa or Australia, though a couple of medals were found lodged in the front pocket of his waistcoat – wrapped up in a silk handkerchief. He liked to dress well. After all, he was betrothed to Toba Sackstein now and on the 28th October, 1908, they tied the knot. Natasha had been forgotten. And anyway, who would want to lie with a woman with consumption?

There was work to be done in the Angel.

PAPA
Recipient of the South African Medal
1901

"The polite black-coated gentleman is enamoured by the ample waist of my grandmother." 1932

Old man Bendel, widower, veteran of the Boer War, passionate seaman, who, as a penniless émigré from Lithuania, had twisted the arm of a sea captain to take him on board, is now Captain of Chapel Market. If he couldn't buy Johannesburg, then damn it, he'd make a mark in Islington.

1932.

The polite, black-coated gentleman is enamoured by the ample waist of my grandmother... Not quite Natasha, nor even Toba, but definitely a consideration. He lays his hand on her bottom and whispers in her ear.

Your name?
Hetty. And yours?
Philip.
Excellent.
Mrs B – we have work to do.
But your wife has just died – and what about the shop?
Number 56? Doris will take care of it.

★

'Powerful cars – crested and flagged – brought civic dignitaries from all parts of London to the brightly lit and decorated Finsbury Town Hall for the annual reception of the Mayor and Mayoress of Finsbury on Thursday... Mrs Bendel cut such a charming figure, wearing an attractive gown of bronze net over satin, embroidered with bronze beads.'[67]

It was the year before the Coronation. I basked in the glory. A proud reminiscence. My mother, Doris, felt differently. To have been taken out of school at the age of fourteen to mind a shop, not least to have her singing lessons curtailed, was not her idea of *pennies from heaven*. But after all, she was now a millionaire's daughter. Why complain?

Her stepfather was the epitome of a rags to riches story – turned down for naturalisation three times, and then 'ending up as the first Jew' to become Mayor of Finsbury.

Philip Bendel and his wife (Mrs B), Mayor and Mayoress of Finsbury, London, 1952

YOU'RE THE TOPS –
YOU'RE A BENDEL BONNET

Islington was dirty – violent and smelly.
Piccadilly, glossy and glamorous.
Ladies needed hats.
Mr Philip Bendel Esq, once a pedlar, always a pedlar, obliged graciously. He would build an empire of hat shops. After all look at his brother – fled Rokiskis, landed in New York and ended up in Fifth Avenue. Was Henri Bendel a relative – did we have roots there? The Cole Porter song[68] had to be the family motto.

★

Early one morning (in the seventies, I imagine), before the black crow and cock screamed out their rude awakenings to the world, Philip Bendel fell from a bus platform in Tottenham Court Road, London.

At his funeral a group of middle-aged ladies gathered around, scurrying together for warmth and comfort; grabbing their polyester scarves for protection against the wind. Poor Philip, 'What a way to die.'

A few yards away stood an old woman, shivering in the cold. She pulled her coat tight across her chest, the thin air causing her to cough and splutter. She was tired. No one knew her or took notice of her. She was lost in the crowd. Quietness descended.

A young boy carrying a prayer book stopped at the crematorium gates and asked the old lady if she was all right. At five-thirty p.m. she tripped over the edge of a tombstone and fell. The following day at her burial, six o'clock to be precise, the funeral director, (a man of little intent) discovered a bundle of letters in her handbag and threw them on the fire.

All of them addressed to the goddess.

CHAPEL MARKET

'These blankets come from Spain, love.
You'd have to pay 60/- for these in the West End. Here's
what I'll do –
To the first lady or gentleman – 45/- no, say, 40/.'

– E.V. Lewis

Alf stands in front of the shop, number 2 White Conduit Street, N1 – murky history. He scratches his head and ponders. Charles Lamb's mother was murdered up the road in 1797, by his sister. And then there was all that stuff about his lover, Hester Savory; the 'fair Pentonville Quakeress'[69] living in his house. Pretty weird family. He hoped she hadn't spread her legs in his cubby hole.

It's a bright day, yet the wind is icy and he tightens the scarf around his neck, burying his hands in his overcoat and stomping his feet hard on the paving stones. He catches a glimpse of children grabbing toffee apples off a stall and hears the chimes of a barrel organ playing olde tyme music, and as to the flower sellers with their straw hats and shawls, well, the very thought brings a blush to his cheeks and he turns for a moment, absorbed in sorting out the sizes of woollen coats hanging on a rail rack in the shop entrance. Alf is a proud man – to think that his family own this entire building. 'Built in the 1830s' his father said, and one morning in the summer of 1922 Shimon, a draper of prudence, who preferred, quite rightly, to be known as a costumier or furrier (so much grander), called upon a Mr J. S. Campion Esq. and enquired as to the cost of building a shopfront.[70]

*

The sun comes out from behind the clouds. Leah calls down from the flat upstairs and stirs the cherry brandy. Juice splatters onto the front of her apron. Alf purses his lips and averts his eyes, unties the string of a large paper parcel. So much to be sorted, knickers and petticoats, blouses and stays, and where will they put it all, that's the question.

Friday evening, before the candles are lit, Leah shakes the breadcrumbs from her apron and staggers over to the bed. Alf sticks his nose inside an old enamel pot and sniffs. Steaming chicken stock, clogged up with masses of carrots and onions, is beginning to boil over. Alf runs his hand through a bush of grey hair, grabs the nearest ladle from the kitchen drawer and scoops out two yellow eggs swimming in the middle. He cuts a slice of bread before the blessing and runs out, fast – searching for the cat.

Maybe –
Leah was never sure.
He would vanish for days.
Nobody knew where he went even when the bombs were dropping.
Twenty years later.
A man inside himself.
When the moon cast its shadow.
You would hear him.
Playing the violin.
Always at night.
Alone.
Solitary.

But on the seventh day of God's week, before the sun has risen or even bruised the sky, Leah gathers the family together, plunges them into water and soap, yells at Alf to look for Hetty, and pleads that just for one day, they all be still.

Shimon, Leah, Hetty and Alf, will rest on the Jewish Sabbath.

They will rise early on the Christian one.

Now sir, I go further than that, for we lose fifty-two-and-a-half days by the early closing of shops as a result of the Early Closing of Shops Bill which your Lordship introduced, making twenty-six more days, and if we were compelled to close on Sundays that will bring the number of days we lose to 169, or an average of three-and-a-quarter days per week.

I sincerely hope that no endeavour will be made to interfere with the religious liberties for so many years enjoyed by His Majesty's Jewish subjects, who would be compelled to work on their Sabbath to save their families from want if this Bill became law. I feel sure that this would not improve us either as Jews or citizens.[71]

Leah pays no attention to aching legs and climbs upstairs into the ladies gallery of Dalston synagogue. She casts her eyes over the congregation, desperate to sit next to Mrs Levy. She will not sit next to Mrs Weinstein. She looks down into the square hall and spots her husband, chatting to Mr Tischler. She prays that they will reach an agreement. The shop needs investment.

And what about the rats –

A young boy recites his bar mitzvah portion. Leah shivers. Her upper lip is swollen. Her thigh is bruised. She fell down yesterday, trying to lift a sack of potatoes on her own. Her husband had left early, gone to see a fur cutter. What a life those women lead, she really shouldn't complain.

But Mrs Levy –
They are shattered.
Machining day and night.
Exhausted.
No ventilation.
Blessed fluff, kills you.
And I'll tell you something else.
I even told my husband.
I am not keeping kosher.
My sister, God bless her soul, won't even drink from a bottle.
Sends us all round to Umberston Street.
What can be better than fresh milk, milked from a cow behind the counter! she says.
Pours it into a jug and knocks on my door at seven in the morning.
I ask you –

Endless, endless stories.
Everyone talking nineteen to a dozen.
I've been invited to a family tea in Regent's Park.

I pull out a tape recorder from my handbag.
I try to pull our lives together.

July 29th 1930
Darling Alf,

I will leave this note with one of the barrow boys, in case you turn up. They all know you.

Your father's business is expanding. He's selling stockings now, travels to Germany every month, rain or shine. I'm telling you, they make the best stockings there. He buys huge quantities of the odd halves of pairs, so as to be able to replace a faulty one. Then he imports them to England and when he gets home, we all sit around the dining table, matching up colours and sizes of odd stockings in size and shade to make saleable pairs. And then he sells them from our stall in Chapel Street, you know the one, on the corner of Conduit, next to the ice-cream shop. Hetty says that on a good day, he can take £100!

But as to how Mr Rosenthal, our neighbour, conducts his business (and I know I shouldn't talk like this) – *Nisht sheymen sich far keinem*[72].

He's set up a pitch in Chapel Street and when someone comes over to the stall to buy a pair of nylons, he only sells them if they've got a pretty face and his wife calls out *'Nicht geht, nicht geht!'*[73] Terrible business. They don't keep any records.

Alf, where are you?

Mama x

Mama –
With the four sons.
The wise, the wicked, the simple and he who hath no capacity to inquire.
I journey to our homeland.
To Dorohoi.

THERE WAS HETTY, JACK, HARRY AND MILLIE

And then Millie's children, Frances and Ossie.
What a crowd.
Squashed together like seven peas in a pod.
In Grandma Leah Cohen's upstairs flat.

It is 1939. Rumour has it that the Germans will land in Newhaven. Hetty's bungalow in Saltdean will have to be evacuated. Frances and Ossie love travelling on the train down to Saltdean and sitting opposite the two sisters, Millie and Hetty. Two sisters in their thirties, more like sixteen-year-olds the way they giggle – Millie especially, she's a real comedienne.

I adored her.

A stray cat wanders into a sitting room. Ossie Landes is snoring, his legs stretched out on an old, squashy, brown leather sofa. God knows where his sister Frances is. Their house in Norbury had been requisitioned by the Council; bodies everywhere, farting and spitting, each one struggling to find a nook to bed down in. As to his grandma's shop in Islington – unbelievable. The flat upstairs is crammed with books and bric-a-brac, a table, piano, candlestick and six chairs. A piece of cardboard is wedged under the leg of the dresser and as to the fire in the grate, well – it's still smouldering.

A violin rests against a music stand and the bombs are dropping all around. Harry, Hetty, Millie and Jack duck their heads and crouch inside a cleaning cupboard. It reeks of paraffin oil. Leah scrams and crawls under the bed. Shimon kicked the bucket years ago.

Alf has disappeared.

LEAH,
YOU HAVE A STORY TO TELL –

I do.
But this one is special.
It is about the fish.

THE FISH

I was talking to a friend one morning. 'I need to do something else in my life' and the friend answered, 'Why not open a fresh fish shop? They do so well. There is always a queue of people waiting to be served.'

Leah asked, 'Where would I go to get the fish?'

'There is a place called Billingsgate Market near London Bridge,' she said, 'but you have to go very early in the morning.'

Next day, Leah left home at the crack of dawn. She walked from Aldgate to Billingsgate Market and wandered around like a lost soul. Suddenly, someone called out to her in Yiddish, *'Leah, voos machts du?'* She turned around and who should she see but a Dorohoi man.

'What are you doing here?' he asked.

'I want to open a fish shop,' she said.

'What do you know about fish?' he said.

'Goornisht!' she replied.

'If you don't know anything, have you at least got a shop from which to sell the fish?'

'Yes.'

'Do you have any money?'

'No.' she said.

The man laughed. 'I'll tell you what, Leah. I'll lend you twenty stone of fish and show you which fish to stock. Pay me when you can.'

And so the shop grew and the debt was paid and everyone was happy.

Hundreds of stories.
Heritage.
Knowing from whence we cometh.

WHEN ALF HAS FINISHED WITH AGEING

He will decide to die.

2014

I had to understand –
To know why he searched for peace on earth.
For a mere snatch of heaven.
Over the tombs of our ancestors.
In Romania.
Dorohoi.

2 WHITE CONDUIT STREET

Leah and Shimon's shop. 2 White Conduit Street, Chapel Market, N1. 1920-1930s.

It was like walking into Miss Haversham's.

Are you there?
I am, my dear. How can I help you?

I duck my head, brushing my fingers along a rack of frayed sweaters and determined not to bump into a tall rack of mismatched clothes hanging above me. The street outside is littered with refuse. Most of the barrow boys have packed up for the night. I close my eyes, thinking of Dad, rushing over to meet him at the shop, sliding on a fallen banana skin, gulping down a glass of orange juice, cutting open a melon, squashing a bunch of grapes into my mouth, throwing away a rotten tomato.

I want to see how Alf lived.

Rosalind sits alone, an abundant lady, greeting me with smudged lipstick and encompassed by twittering budgies, junk furniture, glitzy necklaces, china dogs, dead bits of fur, evening shoes from the forties, and endless scraps of material and rolls of cloth. A vintage leopard skin embodies her frame. Her cheeks are rouged and robust, her eyes, blackened to the hilt. Her mouth gapes open with recognition.

Lionel's daughter!
Yes.
She squeezes my cheek with gusto, snorting with laughter and brushing away a wisp of hair from under her nostril.

Tell me about Alf.

Always running away!
A tramp, sleeping in his raincoat, in utter squalor.
Family should have cared for him more.
Never washed.
No toilet.
Used a bedpan.
Emptied it in the drain over there.
Lived alone for twenty years.
Stacking up newspapers.
Willy-nilly.

Never said much.
Sold nylon curtains.
Made a living.
It was horrible, horrible!
'Cohen's dead and buried,' they shouted out.
Horrible.

He outlasted his mother, as is God's will, or desire. Leah Cohen, widow of Shimon Smaie Cohen, passed to heaven 4th April 1960, in the Metropolitan Borough of Islington. Alf stuffed her clothes into a cardboard box and hid them under his bed.

I shudder.
My brother lives alone.
Avoids the world.
A pattern repeating.
I want to hear all the stories, I want to know.
Because if I know, I might not repeat.
That sense of 'cut off'.
Inside me.
Like Alf.
A wanderer –
Rootless.

THE ROAD TO DOROHOI

AN INNKEEPER TELLS A STORY

Stamford Hill

2011

'In the Eastern European shtetl culture, indiligence and destitution created competitive relations that often out-weighed any other social values, such as solidarity and kindness, but the Innkeeper was Lord.'[74]

In Dunsmure Road, on the left, there are eight shops.

The first specialises in pre-packed meat and poultry, the second sells you medicine. The third posts your letters and the fourth is a grocer. The fifth offers you candlesticks and the sixth, books on the Torah; the seventh is a fruiterer and the eighth sews dresses for your daughters.

On the right is a butcher, a baker and a betting shop, and at the far end, a transport cafe and fried fish factory. Shosh screws up her nose whenever she walks past.

Mr Goldenstein wraps up her potatoes and broccoli in a piece of old, torn newspaper and stuffs it into a plastic bag. Slams the till shut and plonks a few coins of change into her hand. The line of bodies is thickening up behind her and everyone is pushing and shoving, trying to get to the front of the queue, trying to get near to the 'Lord' of Dunsmure Road.

May I ask you a question, Mr Goldenstein?
You may.
Do you know about the flour men, Mr Goldenstein?

My dear young lady –

On the Cantaczino estate in the borough of *Podui Iloae*[75], in the winter of 1836, there lived a number of important folk:

A tax collector and bar owner and even a wagoner; a grocer and glassmaker living with rent and a man who made brandy who owned his own house. There was a cattle trader and butcher who lived in the inn, a helpless old man losing his sight and a widow pleading for charity. The old man was vicious and never paid his rent and, under his bed, kept a pile of coins.

Across the way was a cotton seller living next door to the candle carrier and at the end of the row, the flour man.

His name was Smaie Fainaru. He was your great, great-grandfather. Fainaru means flour man. And as you say –

Mr Smaie Cohen (Fainaru) was a flour man too, I believe. Known by your family as Shimon.

★

Shimon and Leah lived outside the shtetl,
on the border between Moldavia and Bucovina.
They were merchants, prosperous and proud.

Half a world away, in the wintry snows of 1896, Hetty Cohen lay fast asleep, wrapped up in a woollen shawl under a blanket. She was six months old. To her right lay her father, Shimon Maie Cohen, and to the left, her mother, Leah Cohen.

Shimon was born and bred in Botosani.

Leah, the daughter of Sloim Landes and Ita Gross, the sister of Sam Landes, Mendel Landes and Osias Landes, wore her prettiest dress to stand under the wedding canopy and wait for the glass to be smashed into smithereens. The chief of the district named her husband Mr Fainaru, for they lived in a flour mill at the top of a hill. It was the highest hill in Dorohoi. Every night Shimon bashed open the door of their bedroom, exhausted, with flour in his beard. Leah spent her day plucking chickens, chopping carrots and frying eggs in butter, until one night the flour mill was burnt. They lost hoards of money that winter. Villagers had recommended that they manufacture sunflower oil, pressing the sunflower husks into cakes for cattle feed. Two tattered ropes swung in unison from the blackened rafters of the mill.[76]

Leah's face froze into a gesture that would haunt her for the rest of her life.

THE VILLAGE MILL

'The mills were like little square, wooden boxes perched on piles above a massive wheel. Sometimes they were for shredding out wool, sometimes for grinding corn. The flour mills consisted only of two immense grindstones; the upper stone had a hole in its centre and a funnel was suspended above it filled with corn from which the seeds dropped. Beneath, a bin caught the coarse, golden flour as it poured from between the stones.'[77]

The innkeeper told me they'd led a simple life. One worked to eat. That's how it was. There was no other reason. Early in the morning, before the sun rose, when the air was still and flat, when the only sound was the screech of a black crow with bloodied beak, Leah and Shimon would hoist themselves into a creaking open-sided cart and ride out of the shtetl to join the peasants in the fields and begin stripping the maize off the cobs. The men were disciplined in their work, walking tirelessly up and down the regular lines of planted corn. The women followed them, bending their backs low to summer earth, paying no attention to a pain in the back or a toe that was stubbed, merely the rhythm of picking up the cobs and assembling them in straw baskets.

Shimon was a patient man, taking care to grind the wheat over and over again, for the finer it was, the whiter it was and if it was pure white, he could sell it at a higher price. Leah baked such sweet egg *challas*[78] on a Friday morning, and even though the creases on her neck were like a cross-section of tramlines spilling out into Siberia, he'd splodge a wet kiss on her forehead at the crack of dawn and whisper in her ear – Sweetheart.

Leah would turn over onto her side, resting her cheek on the pillow and gripping the blankets tight under her chin, her fingers, gnarled and arthritic, her legs, puffy and swollen. Sunlight filtered onto the furrow of her eyelids. She grimaced, scrunching them up even tighter, not ready for the toil of the day. Two more minutes –

She would haul herself out of bed, swill water between her legs, light the kerosene lamp, for it was still dark and open the door to get rid of the smell of cabbage soup. Then she would bundle herself up with bags and baskets and carry Shimon's boots to the cobbler. He lived down a narrow lane, at the bottom of the hill, beside ditches that smelt, just round the corner from the butcher, next to the *felcher*[79] and fishmonger. She would take care not to trip.

On the way home she would purchase a boiling fowl, and take care (always) to follow Shimon's instructions.

Check the fat, Leah,
and the weight.

That's when the haggling began. She'd take a deep breath, tightening the knot of her scarf around her head and spreading her hands out wide in the air.

Ce vorbesti? Dai un bluz shar'n sus'. Mai mult feidern decat gaina![80]

And when the sun dipped down into the fold of a late afternoon she would pull out parsley roots from a patch of earth and muse for a moment, breathing in the sharpness, the piquancy, of a herb she had grown herself and then she'd sigh and open the door into her house, built on the side of the mill, its walls filled with wattle and daub, its living room, with rag-plaited rugs and to the side, behind an open porch, a work room filled with a baking oven, at least nine feet by six, whitewashed and built of stone.[81]

★

Dear Leah,

I drag myself out of bed, throwing the quilt on the floor and with eyelids half-closed, walk over to the bathroom. I do not light a kerosene lamp. But the kitchen still smells from the evening before, casserole not cabbage was cooked in a pot and I too will walk down to the village. Merely a century of time between us –

The garden is swamped with an early morning mist and a train rumbles in the distance, from over the bridge and a mother shouts at her child, rough and horrible, and two blackbirds descend on the branches of evergreen at the far end of the lawn and I try, try so hard to remember –

Shosh.

IN 1900, SEVERAL GROUPS OF IMMIGRANTS LEFT BOTOSANI BY FOOT

Fusgeyers[82].

Smaie (Shimon) Fainaru, the Flour Man, was not one of them.

He'd got out two years earlier, left Dorohoi, bundled his family into a cart, stuffed their belongings into a sack and trotted off, looking for a train to London.

ROMANIAN PASSPORT
OF MR SMAIE FAINARU
FOUND AMONGST MRS HETTY COHEN'S PAPERS.
FAINARU?
But his surname was Cohen?
FAINARU is Romanian for
FLOUR MAN.

Ministry of Foreign Affairs
In the name of
His Majesty
Carol I
King of Romania.
Request to the civilian and military authorities to allow
Mr Smaie Fainaru
Romanian subject from Dorohoi town
to leave Europe for family reasons and pass freely and to afford him assistance and

protection as may be necessary.
Age: 30 years.
Height: Average.
Hair: Red.
Eyebrows: Brown.
Forehead: Average.
Nose: Average.
Beard: None (shaved).
Cheek: Round.
Face: Reddish.
BEARER'S SIGNATURE:
Minister: D I Ghicanu.
This passport is issued to our best beliefs and is valid for nine months and is good for
departure and return in the country.
Chief of Division: Th. I Zamfrirescu.
1898

★

The sky darkens and the night grows. Shosh is cold. Her body shivers. She rubs her arm to get warm, to get rid of the goose pimples –
A relic of cancer.
A sign.

She spoons manuka honey into her mouth, allowing its sweetness to embrace her. She speaks to the man who is still her friend at the end of a telephone. Maurice is changing his clothes, tucking his shirt into corduroy trousers, pulling his vest down underneath, and getting ready to walk to *shul*. She turns the computer on and surfs the net, searching for more information that will take her back to nineteenth-century Dorohoi. The papers on her ironing board are stacked up into piles, encased in plastic covers. Everything filed and labelled. She has to finish the story; to dig deeper, to complete a past that is merely a root to the unknown, yet gives her a sense of belonging to something bigger than herself. It diffuses the lack of intimacy. But it's difficult. It goes back so far. Her throat hurts.

THE SKY WAS BLACK DEVOID OF LIGHT

Seven a.m.

The men gathered for Minyan[83]*.*
Maurice prays.

DEPARTURES

They arrived early at Luton. The Blue Air desk was not yet open. Maurice and Shosh sat down for breakfast. She glanced at his face, absorbed in the process of shoving granola into a mouth that rarely kissed her –

It was going to be a long day. Why was it, after spending the whole of Tuesday evening in front of the computer, printing out tickets galore, they still ended up last in line and nearly missed the plane?

She sat on the end, by the gangway. Easier to get to the loo that way. Maurice sat squashed in the middle, trying to communicate with the young Romanian girl sitting next to him. But she wasn't having any of it. Her make-up was bizarre, far too much black on her eyebrows and as to her pink lipstick –

But they flew in the sun above the clouds and when they landed in Bucharest it was warm and Shosh touched Maurice's arm in trepidation. She didn't even know what Dan, their guide, looked like.

Maurice.
I bet a million dollars he has a moustache.

She couldn't believe it. Felt like a Third World airport with one luggage carousel.

We take the standard of our lives for granted, Maurice.
We're spoilt, bloody spoilt.

She let go of Maurice's hand, dived through a pair of sliding doors and rushed over to some woman sitting cross-legged on the pavement, dress spreadeagled around her, selling earrings and necklaces to all and sundry. Shosh fancied she'd point her in the right direction as long as she was prepared to buy a bracelet or two. She needed to pee, needed a toilet fast. There was pressure in her bladder area and she was convinced they'd had too much sex the night before.

Maurice was unpacking and repacking his holdall for the thousandth time. He was convinced that a Dan would never materialise and that the whole journey was quite ridiculous. She could hear him now, mumbling on about her impetuosity, hiring an expensive guide to take them from one end of the country to the other in less than five days and on top of everything, the blessed man had the audacity to be late.

At twenty past two the man turned up. Maurice was relieved, pulled a grubby handkerchief from his pocket, blew his nose, and started to tell a story. Life was beautiful. How else could it be? Peace on earth. The man was delightful. He had arrived, he had a moustache and he knew what he was doing. The dear Lord, according to Maurice, forgave us for all our trespasses.

Dan had gone to the wrong airport.

Shosh.

Yes, Maurice?

Didn't you tell him where we'd be?

Shosh smiled sweetly at the man. Now, two men to please.

Dan braced himself. Picked up the cases, hurled them into the boot, shook Maurice's hand at least five times and with delicate propriety asked –

Who is going to sit in the front?

The journey started. Maurice pulled a disc from a leather pouch and asked Dan to insert it into the CD player. Dan pressed the wrong button and air conditioning blasted air onto Shosh's swollen legs. She smiled, imagining for a moment she was at the top of Masada, dancing in the shadow of rocks aged by sand, dust and the histories of decrepit civilisations.

Tell me more about your life, Shosh.

The hairs stood up on Shosh's neck. She could feel Maurice listening. She sucked in her bottom lip, tried not to bite. She must focus.

The journey started. There was nothing to see but Shosh knew that they were leaving Bucharest and heading northwards. They pulled up at a petrol station to fill the tank. Maurice yanked a hundred and fifty lei from his wallet. When they left, the pair of them had a sense that they'd be paying for every aspect of Dan's participation on this journey, even his visits to the toilet.

Just relax, Shosh.
Yes, Maurice.

ON THE ROAD

A sudden sheet of rain lashed down onto the windscreen. Dan frowned. One of the windscreen wipers wasn't working.

Last night Shosh and Maurice danced in Sinaia, a plush hotel owned by a local Jew at the southern edge of the Carpathian Mountains. Cobbled streets and antiquated Latin houses interwoven with wooden verandas and slated roofs stood alongside Christmas fir trees thick in foliage, all cramped together, plummeting down into a land of endless plain.

Shosh and Maurice dressed well for dinner, pulling out crumpled clothes from a battered suitcase and charging around, exhausted, in half-naked glory.

Both of them trying to make an effort.

Shosh locked the room hurriedly and put the plastic key into a small zipped pocket at the back of her bag. Yesterday Maurice had lost it. Today she was taking no chances.

At one of the round tables, dressed with embroidered cream cloth and matching serviettes, Maurice scratched his head; he was quite bald on top now yet to her pleasure still carried bits of grey fluff on either side of a face that was handsome, twinkly and ageing. Yet she turned her face away, irritated by his preoccupation with blessing the bread and only consoled by smiling politely at the waiter, thanking him graciously for the *hors d'oeuvres* and watching Maurice plunge a spoon into a mixture of yoghurt, cream cheese and boiled cauliflower.

As usual, Maurice claimed that such food was too stodgy for his indigestion and with no qualms at all, dug his fork into her side salad of peppers and mushrooms. He always wanted to share her food, rather than order his own. Did he need a mother? The price of staying with him was to put up with him.

I have a delicate disposition, Shosh.
Very small tummy.
Yes, Maurice.
I know.

Dan Jemaro sat next to her, dressed in a clean white shirt and a linen jacket. She could picture his wife, pulling his ties out of the drawer, contemplating the colours and patterns, deciding what would be best for impressing an English client. Dan was the son of an army man. His hair was straight, greasy, greying on the edges and badly cut. Tonight he had shaven, in honour of their company. He lifted his hand up to call a waitress, clicking together the thumb and middle finger. He'd ordered eggs and spinach for a first course. He demanded risotto for the second.

What a journey it had been. Shosh had sat in a grey Chevrolet non-automatic all day. Her legs were stiff and her backside was sore and as to maps, Dan didn't believe in them. When they were in the middle of some godforsaken town, he swerved round the roundabout three times and looked out the window for God before deciding which exit to take.

The music on the radio was crass. He would move the dial of the heater to hot. Shosh would turn it down. He would say nothing and then they'd have a burst of conversation. His English was fluent, his knowledge of Romanian history impeccable.

Interesting man.
Yes, Maurice.

Shosh always sat in the front; Maurice sat in the back, peering occasionally at his book on the Kabbalah and then having a mystical moment, a kind of take-five spiritual get-away. He wore a beige duffel coat, pimpling with age; a woollen cap on his head and an Oxbridge scarf around his neck. Shosh liked that. But on the other hand, he agitated her. His beard had grown longer. His eyes were strained.

What are we doing this for, Shosh?
I want to know where I come from, Maurice. You know that.
I want to find the tombs of my ancestors.

The evening drew on. Conversation, tottering on the border between a belch and a grunt, diminished. Dan Jemaro swallowed his last mouthful of coffee in haste, fondled his moustache, patted his stomach and clicked his heels.

Time for bed.

He was so insensitive, this man. Last night Shosh had to wait until he pulled the chain and left the bathroom. It was not what she'd imagined, a breakfast in cardboard boxes and three people all sleeping in the same apartment. Maurice should know better. He knew how she needed to run to the loo the moment he was finished with all his fiddling.

A hug would have been nice.

TRANSYLVANIA

It is a different hour. A ball of orange sun hovers in the background. Soon it will burst upon them and they will discard hats, gloves and coats indiscriminately, if only for an hour, and ask Dan to park under that clump of trees, just before the mist rises, just so they can soak up the view.

Maurice ambled over to the left.
She to the right.

★

The road is dusty. Three peasants sit in a wooden cart which has come to a halt. They huddle up for warmth. Their dresses reach down to their ankles. A whimpering child crawls out of his mother's skirts and crouches down to urinate; she strokes his head and speaks a foreign tongue. In a field across the way, a bedraggled woman with a walking stick pulls at her sleeve and talks to a half-naked boy, picking at his nose; her bare legs are riddled with varicose veins, her stomach is swollen.

Elte bobe.
Leah.
Did you clutch hold of my great-grandfather's waist and bury your head in his shoulder?
The journey was long and raw to the Port of London.

From Dorohoi to Hamburg.
From cart to train, from ship to shelter.
The poor Jews' temporary shelter[84].

CASTLE BRAN
A fairy-tale fit for a queen.

The afternoon clouded over. Dan wound his way up the steepest road imaginable, pulled on the handbrake and ground to a stop. Maurice's jaw fell open. There it stood, monumental, perched on the top of a hill like a stage set, carved and manicured. The sky was pierced by two steeples, that rose majestically from the blackened walls of a fortress, fingered and touched for centuries in the pages of fairy tale books, in the stories of Dracula.

Shosh loved clambering up and down the staircases, running down passages that wound mysteriously into alcoves and arched doorways; and then she was in a chamber, wide and spacious, its flagstoned floor covered with richly coloured, hand-woven rugs, and its huge double bed pushed up to a whitewashed wall, simply embellished by a dark brown wooden shelf holding a vase of chrysanthemums. Timbered balustrade balconies allowed her to play the fool, to be the medieval queen.

Maurice plonked her down by a niche in the wall, clicked on the iPhone and told her not to close her eyes.

Maybe he did love her.

A flash of lightning cracked open the sky. Rainwater trickled into an outside drain. Shosh wanted to step inside the stone walls and never come out.

BAAL SHEM TOV
(Master of a Good Name)

It was the simple and harsh mountain setting that provided the basis for a movement that deeply affects Jewish life to this very day. This movement is Hasidism. Its founder was Rabbi Israel ben Eliezer (1700–1760), better known as the Baal Shem Tov (Master of a Good Name)… Most scholars agree that the father of this modern movement of religious piety was influenced by his Carpathian mountain environs. His humble beginning, his prolonged seclusion in the mountains and his passionate concern for humans and animals are all characteristic of an individual close to nature.[85]

So the founder of Hasidism was a man of the earth – She liked that. Kind of summed up their struggle. Maurice always needed words to thank God. She was just happy to plant daffodils.

The journey continued. Dan never took his eye off the road. His face was expressionless, as unmoving and hard as the asphalt below them. Clouds of dust hung ominously over stripped fields. The sun fell. Telegraph poles faded into distance. The world felt dull and melancholy. Maurice heaved over.

Okay.
You sit in the front.

And then she leant forward, jolted by the noise of stones and rubble and the road was winding higher and higher and finally she saw them, misty grey peaks, blending into an endless sky – miserable. These were the Carpathians.

BRASOV

A gust of cold wind slapped her in the face. She edged up closer to Maurice, burying her hand into his coat pocket, curling fingers around fingers, saying nothing –

The Black Church of Brasov towered in front of her. Autumnal leaves fell by the ancient walls. A boy ran past, waving a lantern in the air. A woman of elegance, dressed in mink, bent down to pick up her fallen scarf and gloves. A scolding parent scooped up a crying child from the roadside.

Ladies and gentlemen.
It is time.
Musicians in black tie scratch their bottoms and settle themselves. A fiddler lifts his violin to his shoulder and closes his eyes. A cellist sits as still as a mouse, waiting to begin. The conductor lifts his baton. The audience goes quiet. The couple in front looked like lovers. The girl was pretty. Slender neck and dimpled cheeks, skin, fresh and youthful. She knew what she wanted. Shosh sighed and lowered her head onto Maurice's shoulder. Tchaikovsky, Rachmaninov, Schumann. The tickets cost 40 *lei*. Maurice paid.

And then they applauded and the clapping rose to a crescendo and the white-haired conductor was bowing and brushing his hand through his hair and the dear sweet white-haired lady sitting next to Maurice plucked at the roses in her lap and her son looked at her with pride and for a second –

Shosh saw it.
Simple, unencumbered, unconditional.

Shosh, you okay?
I'm fine Maurice, just fine.

Maurice touches her knee, but there is no response. He withdraws gently into his own swim with the music. Her head descends again to rest on his left shoulder; a subtle dance of closeness and separation.

ROMANIAN HILLS AND CORNFIELDS

The harvest is over. Nothing left apart from miserable fields of broken stalk and the muddy tracks of some poor soul's attempt to plough. The sky is grey, the villages, unspoilt. Churches date from the twelfth century. Dan is frustrated, trying to overtake a combination of two trucks and a tootling horse and carriage. Furrowed fields and distant hills take over the landscape. Railway lines appear from nowhere. Telegraph poles run in diagonal lines and are difficult to count.

Maurice complains about his back pain and his bowels. I complain about my legs.

Huh –
Maurice?
What?
Did you pack the medicine cabinet, Zimmer frame and bath chair –
Shosh!

The man is not amused.

But soon the world is glorious again and dear Maurice is purring, literally purring as we wind our way up through forests of fir, low-slung tumbling clouds and powdery snow. A truck laden with felled fir trees misses us by two metres. Maurice ducks his head. I grab hold of the gearstick. Dan swears.

The afternoon drags on. Five more hours

of vehicular madness, purchase of woollen jumpers, woollen socks, woollen hats and woollen gloves. Maurice's stomach is spilling out. Dan swerves round bends, overtakes cars with speedy acceleration and brakes at unanticipated obstacles, trying to gain time. We're not keeping up with his schedule.
It's so blessed tight Maurice.
You tell him you need an extra half hour in the morning to lay *tefillin*[86] –

A train passes, barriers lift; we pass through a railway crossing. Maurice finishes off a packet of tortilla crisps. Another hour to go. We drive on through darkness. Hotel Splendide is our destination. I love it when he turns the iPhone off. I always have the feeling that he is never here; either he's up in the clouds or pontificating to the club.

Stamford Hill darling.
The aristocracy of our heritage.
The umbilical cord.
Can we cut it.
Just for one week.
ONE WEEK –

I cannot do what he wants me to do.
So he must do it for me.
His God is for prayer and song, regular as clockwork.
Mine merely moves with the wind.

Maurice if that's not enough –
It's all right Shosh.
It's all right.

The car rumbles on.
We sit in silence.
He merely taps me from behind.

HOTEL SPLENDIDE

Heritage is our history.
Our belonging –

So this is Dorohoi.
We have arrived.

Yes, we have arrived.

Is this it?
Yes, this is it.

Dan was flummoxed. He had absolutely no idea where to go. The hotel receptionist didn't have a clue. The dining room was empty, the curtains were drawn, the decor – despondent. It was quite obvious; we'd be left on our own to ponder on the ramifications of nineteenth century Jewish history in Dorohoi.

Come on, let's go Dan.
But we've just arrived.
Doesn't matter –
We'll dump our bags and ask a local driver to help us.
We need to find the old synagogue.
Now.

Maurice fastens up the top button of his coat, wraps a scarf around his neck, grips hold of Shosh's hand and gives the driver a tightly folded piece of paper. Dan sits in the front. Shosh and Maurice in the back.

The driver raises his eyebrows at our persistent questioning. Dan interprets. He has an excellent command of the English language, never misses a trick. The driver gives Dan a blank look and shrugs his shoulders.

Okay, we will go there.

The address written on it leads us to a deserted Jewish office. The brickwork is crumbling. Windows are boarded up with iron grilles. A pigeon swoops down and pecks on the turds of a dog, or is it a cat? All we see is a piece of card stuck on the front door with masking tape.

The synagogue is not in use any more.
A vanished community.
It was built in 1790.
It stands in Piata Unirii Street, number 5, Dorohoi.[87]
It lies in the country of Botosani.

Shosh nudges Dan and whispers from behind:
Can we go there –
Now?

Now!
Shosh.
This whole journey is ridiculous.
Where, or what, is it going to lead to?

I don't know, Maurice.
I don't know.

With a rather embarrassed smile, having been so cold in manner to the receptionist less than an hour ago, Dan, who by now was losing patience with our rather amateurish efforts to connect to ancestry, mumbled a few sentences of Romanian to some snoring booking clerk slumped over the counter and, to Maurice's immense surprise at the audacity of the man, admonished us to our room. Was the man planning a threesome?

Who is in charge here Shosh?
Us
or him?

How can Maurice confess to the other side of his experience –
The irritation expressed by his skin.
The invasiveness of Dan.
The sense of oppression by the continuity of this man's presence.
The comfort in reading the Zohar and saying morning prayers.
Living with all the questions.
The ambiguities.
Yet he has to confess.
Dan knows how to make money.

The bedroom assigned to us needed decorating. The lavatory had seen better days. Maurice opens my suitcase and rummages through my clothes, pulls out a red striped dress, throws it in my face, squashes his finger on my nose, pinches my backside and tells me to hurry up.

Come on, let's give up on Friday night.
We haven't got any candles.

He pushes me out of the door and five minutes later is pushing me over to the centre of the dance floor. Downtown in Hotel Splendide –

The booking clerk rushes over to switch on an ancient music centre. He grabs hold of a cloth to dust the speakers. A lone woman with drooping breasts throws back a glass of vodka, into a mouth that is over-lipsticked and looks at us with disdain. She picks desolately at a plate of caviar, left on the bar counter from the night before.

We move well together. We enjoy the rhythm, the movement, the shift between closeness and distance. Tonight Dan leaves us to it.

Maurice enters me from behind.

At ten p.m. I lower my face onto his tummy and rub him gently. He is a good man.

A sharp prism of light throws shadow across to the corner of a room where two people lie huddled together. At seven a.m. one rises and walks over to the shower. The other watches. One gets dressed and says morning prayers. The other merely tugs at the window and opens her mouth to breathe.

Are we an item, Maurice?
Are we?

But at the breakfast table they joke and it's minus four in the sunshine; families traipse in, bundled up in overcoat and fleece, waiters tiptoe round, holding trays of Romanian tarts and trying not to fall, businessmen sit glued to mobiles even on a Saturday and Maurice and Shosh make up stories, ridiculous stories, whilst waiting for their food. When it comes, they eat fast. They promised to meet Dan in the foyer at eight. He likes an early start. The coffee is steaming and the omelette is dry.

Don't rush me Maurice.
Shosh, I'm not rushing you.

THEY ARE LIKE SHELLS ON A SHORE[88]

She searches in vain –

The cemetery lies just outside of Dorohoi on the road to Suceava. We crawl at five miles per hour along an unkempt stony track. My stomach is pounding. Maurice is silent. Dan chews on gum. We grind to a halt.

I get out of the car and stand for a moment, watching. This is a world that sweeps across six acres of dishevelled land and holds five thousand bodies.

Dead ones.

The three of us clamber over a stone wall and enter a field of haystacks and tombstones. In the distance I hear only cows and squawking chickens. Maurice tightens his grasp and pulls me over yet another stone wall. I pick at wild yellow flowers with seeded heads and then I shout at him to follow me and we're running over to the other side, for there they are, hundreds of them, scattered amidst weeds and nettles, tomb upon tomb, tilted and broken, on top, beside and underneath, all of them soiled and half hidden by a mountain of thistle that pricks when you touch it, desecrated by cow dung, spoiled by bird shit, buried, in earth, dust to dust –

I stand in front of a headstone, reading out aloud the names of the deceased. I slide my hand across old Hebrew letters, trying to discern the names of families long gone. I miss my footing, stumble back into arms outstretched, laughing at my clumsiness but at the same time dragging my hand across eyes that are wet.

I hate these places.
Shosh –
Are you ok?
I'm fine, Maurice. Just fine.

The caretaker walks over to greet us. Four small, bedraggled boys walk beside him. They wear shrunken sweatshirts and loose tracksuit bottoms. One picks his nose. Another scrapes mud off his shoes with a knife that is rusty. The third picks at a scab on his knee and the fourth clutches hold of his father's hand. I think of the four sons, the wise, the wicked, the simple and he who hath no capacity to inquire.

I stare at the man's face.

Alf –
Alfred Cohen?
You look like my great uncle.
Booba's son.
Elte bobe.

THE LONELY DEATH OF ALFRED COHEN
Aged
83

'Murder shock waves ran through Islington Chapel Market last week after Mr Alfred Cohen, at 83, its oldest shopkeeper, was found dead in the flat above his White Conduit Street business'.[89]

The caretaker shrugged his shoulders and plunged two hands back into the sleeves of a torn overcoat. He pulled it tight across his chest. The sun disappeared behind a cloud.

You sold bric-a-brac.
Police came round at five p.m. and found two men inside your shop.
Number 2.
Took them to King's Cross.
Released them after questioning.
Detectives suspected you might have been killed in a robbery.

But murder was ruled out.
Post mortem revealed that you'd died of a heart attack.

You'd been mugged.
Knocked out.

The caretaker utters not a word.
He hands me a piece of paper.

The *Islington Gazette* wrote about you!
Friday June 10th, 1983
Mr Cohen's much-talked-about death seemed out of keeping with the lonely and isolated life he led. He was unmarried, but had a brother who came to Islington last week. Police said he lived alone in squalor and had no visitors. The shop had fallen into a poor state of repair and was for sale. But the sign saying 'S Cohen, costumier and furrier' pointed to a more prosperous past.

Chris Painayi, owner of the menswear shop Legs and Arms, had seen Mr Cohen opening up on Wednesday morning. He and his assistant frequently helped Mr Cohen with his shutters, but he seldom said much. Said Mr Panayi, 'He lived in a world of his own. He was very quiet and if he had problems he never shared them.'

Mr Cohen's hours were erratic and he did not trouble to look after himself. He had been in White Conduit Street as long as anyone could remember, since well before the war. We cannot speak too highly of the man. Chapel Market has not only lost its oldest shopkeeper but a character who cannot be replaced.

The lost soul who got noticed.

The caretaker rubs his hand across his eyes and turns away from me, stamping his feet on fallen bracken and pulling a misshapen brown woollen jacket tighter across his chest. He shoves a grimy hand into a leather pouch slung over his right arm. A knitted hat falls low over his forehead. His trousers are splattered with mud.

Please.
We are looking for Smaie Fainaru.
My great-great-grandfather.

He shakes his head and scratches his chin and whispers that he is a man of the Christian faith and turns to the Bible before the sun is down and cares for his wife who is not eating well. And not to forget he is an honest man, and plants potatoes and turnips, spinach and beetroot and though his wages are very low, there is always enough to put on the table and he likes to read before he turns out the light and he is sorry and shamed that we cannot find our loved ones. He is writing the names down of all the poor souls who are buried here. He will even dig up the graves that have sunken into the ground. That is his task –

It will be an honour.

He bends down to pick up a shattered fragment of pottery, filled with black ash and torn tissue paper; the remnants of a stranger's mourning. And then he is rummaging in his pouch for his notebook and showing me the pages, page after page with columns of names scrawled illegibly in blue ballpoint and ripping a page from the back and writing his name and giving me his address and telling me to write to him and beaming with pride at having met me. He takes hold of my arm and pulls me over to a hawthorn tree. The sky is painted turquoise.

Maurice clicks on the iPhone.

The caretaker ambles back to the cowshed, a small ramshackle building, hidden under the trees; shafts of sunlight filter down from a roof, half filled with slats of splintered wood and strips of battered metal.

Maurice and I waited, resting our bodies against the stump of a tree and then we saw him, standing under the spiked branches of a sweet chestnut tree, rubbing his hand up and down the polished maple, stroking it, caressing it like the pungent-smelling skin of a newborn babe, and placing the fingers of his left hand tight against the fingerboard and drawing the bow, horsehair, sharply across three strings, and then plucking three times – *Mayn faygeleh.*
Like Alf.
He closed his eyes in rapture.
I have everything –

Maurice places his hands in between my legs for comfort. The caretaker is a rich man. A millionaire's pauper.

The world moves back a generation –

The glow of a late afternoon sun warms my back. A thin spiral of smoke wisps up into the air from smouldering embers; the remains of a fire built to nourish. Four baked potatoes are handed out to the boys. They shuffle around, quarrelling, not quite knowing where to put themselves. The caretaker peels off his jacket and throws it carelessly onto a patch of moss, vivid green in the sunlight. He leans back, against the hawthorn tree, closes his eyes and starts to tell a story –

The noise of the wheels trundling towards the cemetery was ominous. The mourners had laid to rest two corpses; each one squeezed into a simple wooden coffin, covered by a black cloth, embroidered with the Star of David and placed on a small platform of broken and split wooden boards. The cart was pulled by two pall-bearers, spitting saliva and sweating profusely. Clouds of dust poured into every naked hole of their bodies – an open mouth, a cut on the finger, an exposed slit on the skin.

The funeral procession began at the house and then continued along an unmade-up track towards the burial grounds. It grew bigger and bigger, villagers joined it from every which way.

Maurice was speechless. It was only a few minutes ago that he'd seen the cart, stashed away, hidden, alongside a disused motor bike.

Two coffins were lifted out and lowered with ropes down, down, down into an open pit. The old, the young, even the incapacitated, surged forward, grabbing spades and garden forks, grasping the handles with frozen fingers, digging into mud that stank and hurling cascades of soil down onto two soulless blighters.

Our mouths gaped open.
And the sun sank.

My mother was given no coffin in the village of *Bet Lechem Haglilit*. She was merely wrapped up in a simple white shroud made of cotton and sewn with white thread without a knot. My sister watched her out of the corner of her eye. She requested that the shroud be lifted from mother's face –
Just for a moment.
The last.

THE FLOUR MAN WAS BORN IN BOTISANI

Every Friday at four a.m., before he'd picked the sleep from his eyes, Smaie Fainaru pressed his penis on his wife's bottom, grabbed some clothes from behind the milk churn, wrapped a scarf around his neck, gulped down a glass of tea, wheeled out his wooden cart, kissed the horse and rode off to market.

My impression of Botosani.
A no-man's-land of brick, concrete and nothingness.

Dan tells me that the town used to trade with Poland and that from the fifteenth century onwards, it was an important centre for the trade of grain and cattle in both Moldavia and Bessarabia.

Twelve p.m. and we have little time. Dan stops at a gas station to fill up with petrol. We get stuck in a traffic jam. Maurice squints up at the sky and peering from the window, takes a picture of a gate. A man in torn trousers measures a fence. Dan puts his foot on the clutch and goes down into first gear. Maurice taps him on the shoulder. Dan takes both hands off the steering wheel. I clutch hold of my seatbelt and pull on the straps. Dan wipes a fly off his nose, unwraps two squares of spirulina and, thank God, agrees to stop. If I don't stretch my legs in five minutes, I don't know what I'll do.

★

And then I'm running up to the stallholders and touching the fruits and mouldy tomatoes, pulling out coppers and grabbing a bunch of parsley and thyme and telling Dan, 'This is for your wife,' but he glances away and shifts his eyes. She's never mentioned.

I stare at the faces of the women, lined and furrowed, a drooping belly, calloused hand.

Is that a caterpillar over there?

Dan tells me to clutch my bag. I play a round of boule with the locals. Maurice pulls me away. I step back, shielding my eyes from a midday sun. I climb back into the car, disgruntled. Dan reverses the car and parks on the edge of a gravelled parking lot. I peer out of the window. Again, a stunted horizon, broken not by smudged trees of a faraway land, but by the utilitarianism of high-rise blocks of flats, endless in number. A scrawny teenager hovers inauspiciously by the gated entrance to a park and immediately opposite stands a flat-roofed building, surprisingly plain. The synagogue of Botosani.

Maurice pushes open the door with trepidation.

I am transported into another world. Old lace embellishes a window. Prayerbooks piled one on top of the other are tidied up by an old man, coughing and spluttering. He stoops. Notices of intent hang on white, plastered walls. A few miscellaneous prayer shawls are shoved into a corner under a bench. Maurice is convinced I will have to sit alone in the women's gallery.

And now it is two old men that open the door of the inner *stebl* and come to greet us, to shake our hands. Welcome, they say, and in less than a second we are sitting on a wooden pew, reciting prayers and singing songs and Maurice is swaying and Dan puts his hat back on and stands to attention. Perhaps his father is standing in front of him and he's ready to salute.

The Torah is read. It is the last *parsha*[90] of Vaira, the story of Abraham and his circumcision. The men turn their faces round and smile. I look over to the left and spy a small table. It is covered with a white cloth. On it rests a plate with sliced sponge cake and to its side at least a dozen glasses of red wine. The Kiddush glasses are so tiny, just enough for a blessing. I long to drink. My throat is dry.

The *musaf*[91].
It's too fast, Maurice.
I can't follow.

A man with no expression hurries over to us and pushes us out, but not into the cold; into the adjoining room, built 175 years earlier and I am looking up at the lofty, painted ceiling, overawed by the splendour, the intricate chandeliers, the pictures of Jerusalem, the frescos dated from the early nineteenth century, at all the zodiac signs and representations of the twelve tribes of Israel and finally at the pinnacle of our divinity – the Ark of the Covenant, elaborately carved, divinely decorated, resplendent in its glory. It arches its back, like a bird, into the sanctuary.

The *shammes*[92] is more officious and expects a donation, even on *shabbas*. He stands on a step beside the outer door, without saying a word, confident that one of us will give him something. I pull out of my purse a hundred *lei* and he barely manages a thank you. I ask him if the donation will be recorded. He does not reply.

I turn my head back to take a last look; a Garden of Eden in colours of turquoise, red and gold. The *shammes* acknowledges the tear in my eye, pulls out a key from his pocket and locks the door. He carries a plastic bag, in non-observant mode, and walks beside us, out of the synagogue, out of the parking lot and across the road to the other side. He strides forward and turns his head towards me –

I went to Haifa once.
To see my daughter.
It was too far.
I came home.

He disappears down a sidewalk, squashed between a sandwich bar and supermarket. The sky is prickled with scaffolding. The road smells of carbon dioxide. We watch him, swinging his plastic bag.

People like him stayed in Botosani.
In Dorohoi.
My lot left.

286 KILOMETRES TO BUCHAREST
Hotel Capital

Has Dan really got an international driving licence?
He's a dangerous man.
But I have to admit
fascinating.

Maurice, he's erratic. For God's sake.
Ssh.
Maurice –

Dan takes his hand off the wheel to answer the phone, goes too far to the edge of the road and brakes so fast that Maurice, spread out on the back seat, desperately trying to compose himself by reading extracts of the Zohar, nearly does a head dive through me and out through the windscreen.

Dilapidated matchboxes, built in the fifties, stand on the edge of towns that have forgotten their history. Branches whip against each another in a flurry of wind. A family poses for a photograph in front of an exquisite red and white eighteenth century building; two of the windows are cracked. They stamp their feet up and down, to beat out the cold. Dan tells us that there is no money here. He pulls a handkerchief out of his pocket and spits into it.

No good worrying, is it.
No, Dan.

Bucharest.
I think of turrets, dungeons and crumbling walls.
Romanian palaces of burnished gold.
Ageing artisans' houses.
Mosques, churches and monasteries.

Not quite.
Ceausescu's murder was quick and precise; a simple bullet through his skull.
Chemical towers disgorge smoke round every corner.
Cats slip unbeknown into oil-slick puddles beneath construction lorries and never come out.
The sun boils over.
My armpits stink.

You all right Shosh?
Yes, Maurice.
I'm fine.

Swing doors swivel us into luxury. A porter walks over to help us with our luggage. A receptionist hooks a pearl earring back into her lobe and asks us what time we would like breakfast. The azure blue carpet is thick and the rugs are Caucasian.

Dan fastens his coat, grabs his hat and rushes back to the car. He's forgotten his mobile charger, left it on the seat. Maurice presses his finger down on the lift button. And then, as if in silence for the Sabbath, it descends and we are pushing the black wrought-iron gate to one side and stepping into a palace of shimmering orange mirrors, behind us, in front of us, above us and below – and I am back in Cumberland Court, Marble Arch, soaring up to the fourth floor, yanking open a noisy, clanging wrought iron gate, ringing the bell of number 49 and Grandma is seated in front of the cocktail cabinet, handing out glasses of sherry and Advocaat to all and sundry. The world sparkles. It is 1952, the year before the Coronation.

Strange in a way I'm trying to complete a story. All I do is go back to the beginning –

Shosh, what are you doing?
I was just looking at the view.
That's all.

Room number 23 on the eleventh floor is small, airless and narrow. Two single beds, pushed together to form a double, occupy the wall facing us; underneath the sash window (which I can't open) stands a mahogany dresser and washstand with cracked enamel bowl. All of a sudden I feel old and exhausted. I need to sleep. It's five p.m. and if we go to bed at midnight, we have seven hours left to see the old Jewish quarter, the Boulevard of Socialist Victory, Ceausescu's palace, and the street where Rodica, my cousin lived, right up until 1950 when the communists took over.

Maurice pushes me down onto the bed and gives me strict orders to rest. He'll come back to collect me in half an hour; needs to hook up to the Internet.

I close my eyes. The smell of petrol fumes seeps in to the room. I hear the rumble of buses and trams, the screeching of brakes and the cries of a child. From one moment to another, the light disappears and all is gone. The room goes cold.

Inside me, a picture – icy, freezing nights, fog,
screams, shouts, cattle trucks and Alsatian dogs.
Bucharest cares not for my romanticism.
Whether it be the curse of the *Shoah*[93] or world
genocide,
obliteration of public elegance, ugly depressive
skies, cranes, building sites, wreckage, scaffolding,
industrialisation,
the yellow dust of an open road
swallowed up
in mud, like our lives –

Maurice is ageing. I recognise the difference in his
face since we met three years ago. He will wake me
soon, rub his finger on my nose.
Maurice.
Where are you?
MAURICE.

A LOVE STORY

Our lives are merely cinema shots of a film hinged together by something which is called language.

TO MAURICE

It was a moment that with hindsight I would
have preferred to live without.
This rage, it gnawed at me, like cancer cells, mutating,
gestating. I had to forget.

★

A bald head is scraped clean, fixed, glued
and pinned to his yarmulke.
A flowing prayer shawl draped over stooped
and aching shoulders.
If I dig a hole in his stomach, will a vengeful
God climb out?
Or will it be a tender one that found its soul on Sinai.
This prostrate man with stethoscope hung from ears
and Aramaic letters stuffed into the pocket of his
waistcoat.
Let me force your mouth open with my singed
fingers and drag the sounds from your mouth.

Maurice stayed in Bucharest; needed time to think. He wrote me a letter. I found it under my pillow, stuffed into a white envelope. He cared for me, but that wasn't enough. We weren't following the same path of the faith.

It wasn't his fault that we didn't match. It was not that he couldn't see me, looking, wanting. It was just that he couldn't imagine us wanting the same. He had to penetrate that which he both wanted to possess and be held by.

So he consoled himself with male friendship, staggered into a bar with Dan, one after another. It was quite unlike him. The two of them, the same. It was the male energy that comforted him. Not God alone. To heal the world, one man at a time. To bring order out of chaos. The order that Shosh yearned for.

Not easy in the world of the divine.

As a mate, Dan was perfect fodder.

He would be blessed. He liked history and he liked money. As did Maurice, the two of them, warriors together. Maurice would be the elder. Time for initiation. A kabbalistic deity.

But as for us, it was never quite right. He was one of those men who gave nothing away until the end and then they break down. Shosh remembered the whimper –

Feeble.

As if he'd been attacked.

No energy to fight it.

No energy to notice her.

'Where will sex get you?' she said. 'Will it ever give you a feeling of joining a woman?' She wanted to think that the world crashed when he entered her. Were they in love or were they in pain? What was it?

What amazed her, as she descended onto the runway at Luton, was the sense of all that massive energy, clawing into her, either loving or hating someone, but knowing that they're still in your life, in the crazy hotchpotch of your life, while you're still here. Maurice would never change. Why should he? He stood in front of her, full on, hands clasped on his tum, like a priest from Tuscany, Umbria or Rome.

But you don't even believe in reincarnation Shosh.
You don't even care!
Why should I believe in that
second time round?

The consultant leaned forward. Striped tailored suit, Savile Row, drumming his fingers on the front of her file, opening it, pulling the clip off, shoving the papers out, clearing his throat, looking her square in the face.

I couldn't care a damn about reincarnation, Maurice.
Being here, once, is good enough for me. Just a few
more years –

So the idea was to find something to do that would
take her mind off it.

It –
That's what she called it.
It.
Imagine a seed growing on a scrap of old flannel inside you.
It swells inside your vagina.
It swims into your uterus.
You stand, poised and sophisticated.
Glass of merlot by your side.
Trying to chat.
To the new one.

*

Maurice.
Yes, Shosh?
Do you know what it's like?
Now?

I do it on my own. I have to. Otherwise I will close up. You know what I'm talking about. There's no blood anymore. It doesn't drip. I put a clean white towel on top of the bed this morning. It's still white. When I cry out, I miss you. Or is it really just the relief that for one split second, I am not asked to be anything other than who I am.
Their story began in Uman.
It was extraordinary. The men flew down the mountain, like snowflakes spilt from a bucket, all in white head coverings, some in *shtreimels*, others white

smocks, all to express the desire for purity. Maurice was squeezed, pushed, like a toothpaste tube, into a union of the divine; his toes crushed and splintered into shingle, watching the men, holding hands, singing, lifting spirits, cleansed in intent at least of sins not expressed, not understood even, and hoping, trusting in a clean slate, in the mercy of an uncondemning judgement. He drank it in.

Without her.

Shosh, there is an echo of who I am in you. But your independence is beyond me.

His body edges over to the left-hand side of the bed. Hauls himself out from beneath the sheets.

Tiptoes over the wooden floor. Shuffles over to the bathroom. Pushes a door open. A door that needs oiling. It creaks. He lifts the toilet seat, splashing urine into the bowl in fast rhythmic spits. It is a signal that he cannot rest, a man has to know first where he is going and then who is going with him.

Maurice.

Too many conditions. I cannot wait for the angel. I picked off my gloves and stood waiting for the taxi to take me home. I had loved but now I was alone. There was nothing I could do. I had told Maurice that it was over. He knew why.

I stretched my legs out, pushing the duvet onto the floor.

If I was with another, when would I tell him?

In the dream Shosh sits alone and ponders. The game is over. She stands up tall and ties the skipping rope around his head. She clasps his hand. She grabs the scissors and cuts fast, fast, fast – deep into the cortex of his skull. Ductal carcinoma in situ, non-invasive. I wasn't going to tell you.

TAKE TWO
LAST SHOT

Darling Laurel,

I write to you with love two thousand miles away.
I am well. Nobody can believe it.
But in reality the cancer is silent –
It is in my spine but gently growing.
I ignore it now.
I have returned to Sherborne.
Maurice is not with me.

I watch the lines of sheep cascade across the fields, like the haphazard strings of a violin, trailing I know not where, like the breath in me today, hot, cold, damp, not dying.

Never, never have I felt so gloriously besieged with an energy that is utterly, utterly indescribable. I raced out of the apartment this morning, hoisting myself into an old black shabby anorak, frustrated that I couldn't fasten the zip, tucking my hair into a frayed woollen hat and running, running out under the arch of the Stables and through the gate at the bottom of the hill and down onto the gravel path that winds its way in lustrous patience alongside the Windrush. Sheep scatter away in awesome speed.

But oh my God, I don't know how to tell you this. I mean it's kind of crazy, ridiculous, but I imagine you presume that baby lambs are white –

Well dirty white, but this one was painted orange, bright bright orange. Who, in their right mind, would take a paintbrush and tip a bucket of orange paint over one of these delectable jumping lambs, crawling under the tummies of their mothers and squeezing the very *kishkes* out of them?

I lower my legs over the stile and jump onto a stony path which leads across the River Windrush. Water gurgles at my feet. The heron stands still and I gasp with pleasure at this scene of England. This is what Thomas Hardy wrote about and Constable painted. I, merely a novice with words, dare not even try to convey, describe, this English beauty of sloping down, sprinkled with yellow buttercups and thistles, disturbed only by the resting, puffing sheep as their young ones, both black and white, suck at their udders and stare with fear at my audacity to come between mother and child.

They nestle and I bend my head in homage to their glory. I thank the Lord that I should be here.

But it is in the early morning when I am submerged by water, my hair pushed up into the shower cap, my back rested, that I am at peace, listening to the black crow and cock, their loud repetitive awakenings to the world, stirring my body into stillness. It is in the afternoon that I fidget, unsure of my direction.

Bleating sheep pour like rainwater down slopes of nettle and dock leaf. The memory of a past pervades; there is an ache at the top of my thigh. There is a disturbance.

Being on the edge with the shadow of cancer inside you, one is forced to learn it, know it, accept it and even resist, but not deny it. And it is that tension, which can, I believe, be transformed into a potent and creative vitality, for the life that is left.

If I die, just know that the book is printed out.
It's on top of the filing cabinet
Underneath the Velux window.
I feel so cold.

ACKNOWLEDGEMENTS

My journey for this book began over twenty years ago. A journey of time that roamed through diaries and jottings on pieces of paper; a jigsaw of memory, a montage of life.

I thank everyone who has helped me, from the bottom of my heart –

With special thanks to:

Frances Wilson and Elke Hannah, from the Birchfield Writing group –
and to family, friends and colleagues:

Neil Bendel, Eugene Blackmore, Wendy Bowker, Laurel Essel, Jackie Gay, Eve and Chris Goldie, Patricia Har-Even, Roger Noble, Christopher North, Kate Riley & Paige Kaye, Professor David Roberts
&
Professor Melissa Raphael who gave me the confidence to stand by my own personal struggles and complexities around Jewish identity and to publish.

Thank you to the Eyewear/Maida Vale team, especially Edwin Smet for his design of the book; and Todd Swift, Alexandra Payne and Rosanna Hildyard for their editorial advice.

ENDNOTES

1 Stuart Handyside: letter
2 Susan: middle name of Carol Nathanson
3 Letters from Jack Cohen (Jacob Tertz): Family archives
4 *Shwartzer*: Yiddish – a black woman
5 *Moshav Bet Lechem HaGlilit*
6 *Aliyah*: Immigration of Jews to the Land of Israel
7 *Kneidlich*: A type of dumpling eaten in Jewish households during Passover
8 *Shabbas*: Sabbath
9 *Bracha*: Blessing
10 *Beshert*: Destiny
11 *Shiksa*: A gentile woman who has attracted a Jewish man
12 *Habonim*: A Jewish Zionist Labour Youth Movement
13 *Moadon*: Clubhouse
14 *Kibbutz Amiad*
15 *Yishuv*: Settlement
16 *Tishon chamud, tishon*: Sleep, my sweet one, sleep
17 *Chader ochel*: Dining room
18 *Metapelet*: Nursery nurse
19 *Kaddish*: Mourner's prayer
20 *Yahrzeit*: The anniversary of a death
21 *Yiddishkeit*: Yiddish culture
22 *Torah*: The five books of Moses
23 *Vayikra*: The twenty-fourth weekly Torah portion in the annual Jewish cycle of Torah reading, and the first in the Book of Leviticus
24 *Shabbas*: Sabbath
25 *Chazzen*: Cantor
26 *Beth Din*: A Jewish court of law composed of three rabbinic judges
27 *Shtibl*: Little room for communal Jewish prayer in contrast to a formal synagogue
28 *Tallit*: Prayer shawl
29 *Siddur*: Jewish daily prayer book

30 *Tsitsis*: Specially knitted ritual fringes or tassels, worn by observant Jews
31 *Tefillin*: A pair of black leather boxes containing Hebrew parchment scrolls
32 *Yom Kippur*: Day of Atonement
33 *Amidah*: The central Jewish prayer
34 *Shul*: Synagogue
35 *Gud yomtov*: Traditional Ashkenazi greeting for a special Jewish religious holiday
36 *Tisha B'Av*: Day of fasting and mourning for destruction of the First and Second Temples in Jerusalem
37 *Get*: Jewish religious divorce
38 *Meshugge*: Crazy
39 Law abrogated by Rabbeinu Gershom in the tenth century
40 *Mechitzah*: A partition that is used to separate men and women
41 *Mazal*: Luck
42 *Davenning*: Praying
43 *Mitzva Tanz*: Chassidic dance
44 *Seder*: Jewish feast, marking the beginning of Passover
45 *Charoseth*: A sweet symbolic food eaten at the Seder
46 *Chassidim*: Strictly Orthodox Jewish sect
47 Hogsback: Village in the Amathole mountains in the Eastern Cape province
48 Mama Tofu: Matriarch, story-teller and keeper of tradition for a Xhosa village
49 *Kishkes*: Yiddish – intestines
50 Sourced from 'The Log of A Sea-Waif' in *The Cruise of the 'Cachalot'*, by Frank Thomas Bullen. First published by Collins, London and Glasgow in 1899. Latest edition:1953
51 Sourced from *Types of the Old Home* by A. Koseff, translated by Gloria Berkenstat Freund
52 *Environs: Abel* by I. Michel-Michalewitz, translated by Nathan Summer
53 *Notes on the Landsmannschaft of Rakishok* by A. Eidelman, translated by Gloria Berkenstat Freund
54 *In the Belly of the Whale: The Journey to South Africa 1880–1910* by Gwynne Schrire

55 *Fress*: Eat like an animal, quickly, noisily
56 *Griner*: New immigant
57 *Shmutters*: Rags
58 *Kishke gelt*: Intestine money
59 Sourced from *The Thorny Path of Jewish Immigration to South Africa* by J.M. Sherman, translated by Rae Meltzr
60 *Smous*: Peddler
61 Sourced from *Book of Memoirs: Reminiscences of South Africa Jewry: Contemporary observations on the social environment of South Africa in the early twentieth century* by N.D. Hoffman
62 *'Vant to Puy a Vaatch': The 'Smous' and Pioneer Trader in South African Jewish Historiography* by Milton Shain
63 Sourced from *A Voyager Out: The Life of Mary Kingsley* by Katherine Frank, published by Ballantine Books, New York,1986, pp. 291-293
64 Sourced from *Book of Memoirs: Reminiscences of South Africa Jewry: Contemporary observations on the social environment of South Africa in the early twentieth century* by N.D. Hoffman
65 *The Boer War*, p.74. (Signed) Redmond Orpen Major Commandant. Draghoender 9.2.01.
66 Philip Bendel: Sourced from naturalisation documents: Criminal Investigation Dept., Metropolitan Police, New Scotland Yard, 24 July 1911
67 *Islington Gazette*, 13th May 1952: 'Colourful Scene At Finsbury - Civic Reception'
68 'You're the tops, you're a Bendel bonnet, a Shakespeare sonnet', 1934
69 Fictionalised extract sourced from *Survey of London*, Vol. 47, 'Clerkenwell & Pentonville', p.395
70 Sourced from *Survey of London*, Vol.47: Clerkenwell & Pentonville', p.402
71 *A Documentary History of Jewish Immigrants in Britain 1840–1920*, ed. David Englander, p.130
72 *Nisht sheyman sich far keinman*:You shouldn't be ashamed of anything
73 *Nicht geht*: No money
74 *Folktales of the Jews* Vol. 2, p.413, 'Commentary for Tale 56'

75 *The Jewish Community in Podu Iloaiei: Pages from the History of a Moldavian Shtetl* by Itzik Schwartz-Kara
76 'Flour mill of Leah and Shimon Cohen, burnt down in pogrom', Dorohoi, Romania, 1896
77 Sourced from *Romanian Furrow* by Donald Hall
78 *Challas*: Plaited white bread
79 *Felcher*: Apprentice medic
80 'What are you saying? The chicken's so light one blow will blow it away; she's more feathers than chicken.' (*Stefanesti: Portrait of a Romanian Shtetl* by Ghitta Sternberg. Published by Pergamon Press, 1984
81 Sourced from *Stefanesti: Portrait of a Romanian Shtetl* by Ghitta Steernberg. Chap. 1, 'Geographic Location'
82 *Fusgeyers*: Jews who fled persecution in Romania in the early 1900s
83 *Minyan*: A quorum of ten men over the age of thirteen required for traditional Jewish public worship
84 The Poor Jews' Temporary Shelter: Founded in 1885 to deal with the large numbers of Jewish immigrants arriving in London's East End from Eastern Europe
85 *Piety and Perseverance: Jews from the Carpathian Mountains* by Herman Dicker. Chap. 1, 'Hungarian Jews from the 18th Century' p. 3-4
86 *Tefillin*: Two long, thin, leather straps, with a two- or three-inch square leather box on each. Boxes contain tiny parchments on which are inscribed in Hebrew four passages from Exodus and Deuteronomy. Tefillin are worn during morning prayers by Orthodox males past the age of bar mitzvah.
87 Gruber, Samuel D. *Historic Jewish Sites in Romania*.
88 *Like Shells On A Shore: Synagogues and Jewish Cemeteries of Northern Moldavia* by Geissbuhler, S
89 Holland, C. *Islington Gazette*, Friday June 10, 1983
90 *Parsha*: Weekly reading of a Torah portion
91 *Musaf*: Religious service celebrated by Jews in addition to and immediately after the morning service on the Sabbath and festivals
92 *Shammes*: Official in synagogue who manages man of the day-to-day activities
93 *Shoah*: The Holocaust

OTHER MAIDA VALE TITLES

Chris Moore – *Barbell Buddha*
Eric Sigler/Donald Langosy – *The Poet's Painter*
David Fox-Pitt – *Positiverosity*
Wesley Franz –*Apterous Dreams and Birds*

Maida Vale is an imprint of Eyewear Publishing Ltd, and is proud to work with authors to develop their rich and complex literary projects, from memoirs to self-help, poetry to novels. Our list is growing, and has so far included artists and poets from Miami and Boston, a famous fitness guru, and a Brazilian scientist-poet.